Glenn Borreson has given us a profound and yet wonderfully accessible book on baptismal spirituality. This pastor gently leads us deeper and deeper into the water of this gift, and in the process he leads us into the heart of the Christian faith itself and into clear proposals about what happens to our lives when this gift is taken seriously. Wade in this water. Drink it. You will find yourself much refreshed.

> Gordon W. Lathrop, Professor of Liturgy Emeritus
> Lutheran Theological Seminary at Philadelphia

Water for Your Soul captured me. Each chapter became a personal experience of God's extravagant love. Pastor Borreson's wondrous book brought Christ close. I will return to it again and again.

> Bishop April Ulring Larson, La Crosse Area Synod
> Evangelical Lutheran Church in America

Parish pastor Glenn Borreson has written a very helpful guide for congregations and individuals to use in an in-depth walk through the many realities of Christian baptism. It is concise, well-written, practical, clear, and full of grace, to mention just a few of its excellent qualities. Here is a very helpful devotional tool to lead readers through the labyrinth of grace that Holy Baptism affords the believer. I recommend it very highly.

> Dr. Richard A. Jensen, Carlson Professor of Homiletics, emeritus
> Lutheran School of Theology at Chicago

Like the miracle of baptism it celebrates, this book is all gift, fully as generous and joyous and beautiful and life-giving as the sacrament itself. In brief, incisive meditations Glenn Borreson leads us on a month-long walk through life as seen through baptismal eyes.... Here is that all-too-rare book that begs to be read repeatedly, as its gracious wisdom washes over the reader with new life each time through.

> Sheldon W. Sorge, Associate Director
> The Louisville Institute

In our identity-confused society, too many of us have settled for a pastiche identity composed of social security number, medical records, academic degrees, job history and whatever fragments of genealogy we can salvage from the cemeteries. Christians can do better: we are *baptized*. Glenn Borreson, working with 36 years of parish practice and reflection, helps us recover our core baptismal identity – an identity that is both clear and profound. And accurate. This is who we are.

Eugene H. Peterson, Professor of Spiritual Theology
Regent College, Vancouver, B.C.

Luther taught us that baptism is the Christian's great comfort in life and death. Glenn Borreson has written a wonderfully Lutheran, deeply faithful book on the joy and the gift of Christian baptism. Pastors, congregations, individual Christians will find new meaning in their own baptism through his fine book. Remember your baptism and be thankful!

Will Willimon, Bishop
North Alabama Conference of the United Methodist Church

The language of God has always been story, symbol and ritual. In helpful ways Pastor Borreson draws upon stories (biblical and personal ones), explores the meaning of baptismal symbols, and suggests simple rituals families can practice so that baptism is understood as one of the most life-giving gifts ever. In an honest and gentle style *Water for Your Soul* makes baptismal connections to text messaging, consumerism, parenting, weddings, Sunday worship, life callings, prayer, and even hand-washing. For those who would like to understand what God is saying in and through baptism each and every day, this book is for you.

Pastor Mike Woods
Evangelical Lutheran Church in America

WATER FOR YOUR SOUL

Living in Baptism Every Day

*For Mike —
for the privilege of our baptismal calling
and for your wonderful support —*

Glenn L. Borreson

*Glenn L. Borreson
February 1, 2008*

Copyright © 2008 by Glenn L. Borreson

All rights reserved. No part of this book shall be reproduced or transmitted in any form or by any means, electronic, mechanical, magnetic, photographic including photocopying, recording or by any information storage and retrieval system, without prior written permission of the publisher. No patent liability is assumed with respect to the use of the information contained herein. Although every precaution has been taken in the preparation of this book, the publisher and author assume no responsibility for errors or omissions. Neither is any liability assumed for damages resulting from the use of the information contained herein.

ISBN 0-7414-4437-2

Bible quotations are from the New Revised Standard Version Bible, copyright 1989, Division of Christian Education of the National Council of the Churches of Christ in the United States of America. Used by permission. All rights reserved.

Cover design by Erik B. Borreson.

Photos: Wisconsin water scenes, by the author.

Published by:

1094 New DeHaven Street, Suite 100
West Conshohocken, PA 19428-2713
Info@buybooksontheweb.com
www.buybooksontheweb.com
Toll-free (877) BUY BOOK
Local Phone (610) 941-9999
Fax (610) 941-9959

Printed in the United States of America

Printed on Recycled Paper

First Published January 2008

Acknowledgments

To The Louisville Institute and Holmen Lutheran Church I owe the sabbatical time for writing these words that have been building and brewing over years of ministry. To Wilfred Bunge I am grateful for editing my manuscript. To Gordon Lathrop and other readers of this manuscript I am thankful for encouragement and suggestions. To Erik Borreson I am indebted for this book's striking cover. To the congregations I have served I owe the Call to baptize, preach, and teach—and the humility and joy of continuing to learn how God is at work. And to my wife Mary and our family I am grateful for love which, like the water of baptism itself, gives life.

Contents

Introduction	1
1. Water for the Soul	4
2. The Inheritance	7
3. Along for the Ride	11
4. Always a Gift	14
5. God Gets Physical	19
6. Dress Rehearsal	22
7. Safe in the Waters	26
8. New Every Day	29
9. God Slept Here	32
10. What the Waters Reveal	35
11. Sleeping and Waking	39
12. Looking Into the Darkness	42
13. Making the Sign	45
14. Jesus Never Comes Alone	48
15. In the Name	51
16. The Rhythms of Prayer	54
17. The Rite Gift	57
18. Real People	61

19. Are We There Yet?	65
20. Through the Waters	68
21. Amazing Beginnings	71
22. Dying to Change	75
23. Letting Go	78
24. More Than Our Decisions	81
25. What the World Runs On	84
26. Spirit Blessed	88
27. A New Holiness	91
28. The Front Line	94
29. Thinking Differently	97
30. Into the World	100
31. Restless Hearts	103
Endnotes	106
Appendix: How to Use This Book	109

Introduction

Water is the gift of life. The water of our mother's womb gave us birth; our spiritual life began in the water of the baptismal font. We cannot overstate the importance of water for human existence. Without water, we would not be here.

This is a book about ordinary water that becomes extraordinary when it nurtures our life with God. Whether in baptism as an infant or as an adult, physical water serves as water for the soul. Its chemical makeup does not change, but it takes on depth and breadth to quicken our spirit, our life with the God of the universe.

As a Christian, I believe that water is the marvelous creation of God, and that the specific water of baptism joins us with Jesus Christ, who reveals to us the heart of God. This bond occurs whether we were babes or advanced in years when the water of baptism washed over us. In other words, what happens is larger than we.

Among the giants of our Christian past, Martin Luther claimed in baptism "every Christian has enough to study and to practice all his life."[1] He lived every day trusting a generous God who continued to give and self-give. He remembered his baptism as a clear word, a very personal word, that God was for him.

But how shall we "remember our baptism" if we experienced it as an infant or a young child? Even if we do remember it and can describe it in detail, how does that memory affect our spiritual life? How does the event of baptism shape my life with God today?

This book is a response to these questions. I believe that baptism is a life-changing event, and the chapters that follow are an attempt to spell out what that means for the ongoing spiritual journey with God, with Jesus Christ, with the body of Christ called the church, and with the world.

Baptism is initiation into the Christian life, much more a beginning than a finished act. Baptism has a cluster of meanings that unfold in our life over time, a spiritual treasury that becomes our own. As a hint of things to come, let me say that baptism has to do with our identity, spiritual confidence, dying and rising, repenting, changes in life, consolation, and engaging the world, to name a few. To remember our baptism is to receive the gift and call that come in baptism by making them our own.

Writers in several traditions have suggested that most of us have only touched the surface of baptism's possibilities for blessing our spiritual life. Tom Troeger called baptism one of the central "metaphors we live by."[2] Maxwell Johnson wrote of the need for a "baptismal consciousness" in our lives.[3] James White observed that "Lutherans have yet to catch up with the depth of Luther's baptismal piety *as a way of life*"[4] (italics mine). The liturgy and worship of the Lutheran church, including the 2006 publication of *Evangelical Lutheran Worship*, indicate a growing appreciation of baptism's central place in the whole life of faith. Lutheran teacher Gordon Lathrop underlines this central commitment when he writes: "A once-for-all event, baptism takes a whole lifetime to unfold."[5] This book is another effort to make the water of baptism flow more deeply into our daily lives.

If you are a baptized Christian, this book will take you back to your baptism. This is my intention, and that you return in such a way as to renew or revive your spiritual life.

If you are not a Christian, or not baptized, this book is an invitation to connect with a Christian congregation as a way of moving on in your spiritual journey. Though all too human, the church is still a place where Jesus Christ, the heart of God, is present.

About reading this book:

I invite you not only to read this book, but to experience it as well. As a spiritual movement into baptism, each chapter encourages you to reflect on one dimension of God's water-and-word event. Some chapters offer spiritual practices for your own life or that of your family. Thirty-one chapters suggest a full month to be immersed in baptismal spirituality. Take your time, don't rush your reading, feel the baptismal water wash you.

At the end of each chapter is a brief section called "Reflections on the Water," with three lines to continue your thinking. In the *haiku* form I have composed spiritual *haiku*. Many view *haiku* as simply lovely pictures in three successive lines of 5-7-5 syllables, but this is unduly rigid. *Haiku* poets do not adhere strictly to a given number of lines or syllables. It is more accurate to understand *haiku*—and their close relative, *senryu*—as succinct moments of heightened awareness in nature or human nature. They are open and suggestive, encouraging us to imagine a scene, what is spoken and what is not. In other words, the reader contributes to the creative process. One author of *haiku* said that he wrote them "to get in touch with the real."[6]

Read each *haiku*, deliberately and thoughtfully, after its chapter. Imagine the scene. Let it take you where it will. Flesh it out with feelings, in the scene or within you. Reflect back on the reading you just completed, especially on connections with baptism. Move into prayer. Use the *haiku* to help you experience God's water for your soul.

1. Water for the Soul

As water for the soul, baptism gives what water itself gives—life.

The doors of the church are open, the lights on, the baptismal font filled with water. The people begin arriving. A few break with tradition and choose the front pews. They are here for the baptism. A small commotion follows; the sponsors were sitting in the wrong place. Everyone settles in, more or less. The center of attention is unwrapped, blanket after blanket. After all, this is Wisconsin in January. In a moment the organist will signal the beginning of a death and life drama.

Is this simply the beginning of a service that includes a sweet ceremony for a lovely baby? Is that the reason all those people showed up? A baptismal rite it is, but never just ceremony and always more than sweet. In baptism, for all its human ordinariness, God has chosen to give us what we cannot give ourselves—forgiveness, life, and salvation. Words and water work eternal purposes. Words this baby will eventually learn for herself. Water she will splash when her mother bathes her.

Baptism is water for her soul, water for her life. Jesus calls it "abundant" life, living that overflows with God. She will get so much of God in her baptism that she will spend the rest of her life learning what it means, what it is to be a child of God, loved by Jesus Christ.

We the baptized sometimes act as though baptism were just a special "do" for infants or children, and then, as with other childish things, we leave it behind. This should not be so. Baptism has a permanent, indelible character. Sometimes we even view it as a relic of the past. Nonetheless, it remains, in spite of us. What we fail to grasp is that baptism is truly water for the soul. It is essential for life, a blessing that endures and does not vanish.

For a moment, consider water. Among earth's most ordinary elements—even one of the ancient world's four—it is essential for life itself. While water covers a large part of the earth's surface, much of it is salt water; just a fraction is fresh. That small percentage is vital to all life. I had an urgent reminder of this when, within hours, an aggressive virus led to a son's dehydration and hospitalization. Water means life.

In the water of the womb life itself develops miraculously. With water we have an answer for our thirst, a shower for cleanliness, and a lake for recreation. At every turn water is part of our lives. We cannot imagine a world without it. It should be no surprise to us that God uses water, so vital to our physical life, to be the sign of our new life in baptism. Water's qualities are life giving, refreshing, renewing. Water is always about life.

Water for the soul, this gift of baptism, declares that we have life in its fullness only in relation to God. Apart from God and life in harmony with God, we do base and self-centered things to each other. We ruin the wonderful life given in our birth. Even so, God loves us—and always has—and gives us another chance in the water of baptism.

What do we get in this water for the soul? We receive life, full and abundant, from the master of life, Jesus Christ. In this water we get everything that belongs to Christ, who in turn gets everything from his Father (John 16:15). So it goes: from God to Jesus, to you and me. This is the "happy exchange" cherished by Luther himself: God gives us the glorious riches of Christ's victory in exchange for the garbage of our sin, so that we might in turn give to our neighbor. How utterly different this is from the world's "religion" in which we give to God so that God is obligated to us. This is a spiritual treasure so great we can spend all our days learning what it gives us.

Let me highlight two key points about this life:

First, a spirituality based in baptism always has its center in Jesus Christ. Its meaning comes from him. When we speak of "water for the soul," we are not speaking of any and all water. This is not a spirituality of water alone, but of water used by Jesus Christ for his purposes in our lives and in the world.

Next, we can never leave baptism's water for the soul behind as though we have outgrown it or have become spiritually superior. Just as we need water every day for life itself, so we continue to need the water of baptism for the soul to flourish. This water concerns our network of relationships centered in Christ. To say that we need this water for our soul is, in the end, to say that we need Jesus Christ.

So this word concludes in the place we began:

The baptism is over. The family finds its way back to the pew. Everyone is happy, in part because baby daughter did not decide that this was a major feeding time. The baptismal water had splashed all around the sides of the font—the pastor was lavish in its use. The last drops evaporate from her dark hair, and soon even her outfit will be dry. Later we will empty the font on an evergreen shrub in the church lawn. For those who have eyes to see, in the midst of these visible details God has washed a soul and a life with Christ has begun. It happens even in winter in Wisconsin.

Reflections on the water:

splashing in the font

everyone completely soaked

God's gone wild

2. The Inheritance

"Unclaimed Money! It May Belong to You!" I saw the headline, again. The State of Wisconsin was holding unclaimed money, and some of it could be mine. I hoped! I checked out the lists, first in the newspaper, then online. All those names and not once did mine appear. No one had left me an inheritance. No one.

Baptism, however, is an inheritance awaiting our claim. That's true. The day of our cleansing at the font marked an inheritance with our name: "You, child of God, inherit everything that belongs to Jesus Christ." Riches so vast that language of description fails us.

We find ways to ignore the good news. We reduce baptism to a charming naming event, and then return home and bury the treasure. Or we sum up the gift's value too narrowly—"Now you can be sure of going to heaven!"—that it doesn't change our lives now. Buried again. Some may even find the baptismal ceremony an interruption in their worship, missing the significance of the new child of God for the life of the entire community.

The Sacrament of Holy Communion is an explicitly personal gift—"The body of Christ for you; the blood of Christ for you." Before this, however, Jesus Christ was *for you* in the Sacrament of Holy Baptism. He was born, lived, suffered, died and rose *for you*. He poured himself out for us, and everything he was and did became ours. Of course, the fact that he rose to new life beyond the grave is why this matters so much; he continues to give in our relationship with him.

I love the passage in the Gospel of John (16:15) in which Jesus announces that he has received from his Father everything he has, and every thing he has he gives to us. He holds nothing back. Baptism is gifting time, and the rest of our lives we live from that inheritance.

What is this gift? We receive all that belongs to Jesus in his triune relationship with the Father and the Spirit.

First, the greatest gift is the presence of Jesus, and, with this, the very presence of God. "For where two or three are gathered in my name, I am there among them" (Matt. 18:20). "And remember, I am with you always, to the end of the age" (Matt. 28:20). We, who long for the return of those close to us when they leave for a time, know what a gift presence is. Jesus' presence is love, love that addresses us in his words and love beyond words. It is healing, the power to mend wounds that have defied other powers. It is union, the yearning of our hearts across all the divides of time and space, even sin and death. Jesus' presence, the living presence of love, is ours, and in him is the fullness of God, Father, Son and Holy Spirit.

Second, we receive the Word. Scripture becomes our heritage. The stories and everything in the Bible become our story, not just interesting history, but pages in our relationship with God. Martin Luther's Flood Prayer ("Through the waters of the flood you delivered Noah and his family, and through the sea you led your people Israel from slavery into freedom. At the river your Son was baptized by John and anointed with the Holy Spirit. By the baptism of Jesus' death and resurrection, you set us free from the power of sin and death and raise us up to live in you."[7]) that Lutherans pray at baptism is a recitation of God's use of water in the saving history of the world. It connects the earth's waters and the water of baptism with the events of all of Scripture. Just as baptism has but a few sprinkles and yet works with power, so the Flood Prayer has but a few stories that connect us with the treasury of the Word. It is all our story from the opening of Genesis, "In the beginning when God created the heavens and the earth" (Gen. 1:1) to the close of Revelation, "Amen. Come, Lord Jesus!" (Rev.

22:20). Scripture is the Word by which God continues to speak.

Third, we receive the Holy Spirit and the gifts of the Spirit. The baptismal prayer from Isaiah 11:2-3 ("Sustain [name] with the gift of your Holy Spirit: the spirit of wisdom and understanding, the spirit of counsel and might, the spirit of knowledge and the fear of the Lord, the spirit of joy in your presence..."[8]) names the gifts that found fulfillment in Jesus, and now come to us in baptism. If you were an infant or young child at the time of baptism, you will not remember this prayer. The promise is God's, however, and God's promise transcends our memory. The Holy Spirit was at work in us before we knew there was a Spirit.

The story of our inheritance doesn't end here, just as it doesn't end with baptism. That is just the beginning. Every baptized child of God needs and receives the community of faith, the church, to gain access to that baptismal treasure.

Consider this story as an illustration of baptismal truth. A very generous grandfather wanted to make certain that his two grandchildren would one day be rich. He made a large deposit in a bank account in their names. He rejoiced as he as he imagined the life they would have. It warmed his heart to think of how overjoyed they would be at this inheritance. One day he died and the money should have come to them. Unfortunately no one informed them of the inheritance, and they never discovered it.

The baptized everywhere, whatever age, need the church community in order to learn of their inheritance and come to enjoy it. We may disagree on whether baptism is effective for infants or children, but the key question is whether the church community that harbors them is effective. Children need other believers to tell the stories, live the Christian life, and share the joy of the Spirit of Christ. Only then can they know and spend their inheritance.

Compared to that "unclaimed money" that caught my attention, this inheritance is everything.

Reflections on the water:
named to get it all
he wasn't deserving, they whispered,
and they were right

3. Along for the Ride

The movie *Dark Territory* offers a window on the world that Jesus entered for us. A train, controlled by evil men with horrific destruction in mind, enters a territory where no communication is possible. The hero, and only hope, confronts these enemies, armed with his ingenuity and strength alone. They are prepared to fight to the death to accomplish their wicked aim. In this film's dark territory we have the cinematic experience of traveling with hope, awaiting the outcome for the world: life or death.

This is a parable of the Christian story. Jesus dies alone on a cross under cruel powers. He is buried and descends into hell, the realm of the evil one. No one has escaped this place; we can expect no other outcome. But on the third day, against all odds, against the ungodly forces of sin, death, and the power of the evil one, this Jesus rises from death to life.

Jesus did not do this for himself. Scripture testifies that he did this for us. He didn't need to go through hell; we needed him to do it. In Colossians we read, "when you were buried with him in baptism, you were also raised with him through faith in the power of God, who raised him from the dead" (Col. 2:12). And further, "for you have died, and your life is hidden with Christ in God" (Col. 3:3). One of the wonderful words in these verses is "with," the simple and beautiful preposition "with."

What does that "with" mean? Jesus took us along into this frightful battle, so that we might share in its glorious outcome. He took us "along for the ride," so that what was his—struggle and victory—might belong to us as well.

What does this have to do with baptism? This water-and-word-event connects us with Jesus in his dying and rising, so that we might have life, life abundant now and life eternal forever. What happened to Jesus happened to us. He was and continues to be our companion in the face of sin, death, and the evil one—anything that can separate us from God. The result is life.

The cost to Jesus was heavy: suffering, pain, alienation, abandonment. Life with God comes at great cost. *Saving Private Ryan*, the movie starring Tom Hanks that is based on a World War II episode, provides an analogy for that sacrifice. A specially assembled team of soldiers has an assignment to rescue another soldier, the one remaining son in his family, from behind enemy lines. They carry out their mission, but at the cost of life to members of their squad. It was the mission that mattered.

Even so, we experience being "with Christ" in his battle and in his victory. Being with Christ is no mere movie experience. It is the deep, pulsing reality of the world we live in. It is the reality of God's passionate care for all creation. "For God so loved the world that he gave his only Son" (John 3:16).

To say that we are along for the ride "with Christ" is not to trivialize what happened, either with Jesus or in our baptism. Quite the contrary. "With" is a term of deep love, of sacrificial commitment. To be with Christ is to be loved as a parent loves a child and will even die for that child.

Being along for the ride is to move from fear and terror to joy and grace. Imagine a father offering a child a ride on a fine horse. She sees the horse gallop like the gusting of the wind; she watches the animal paw the ground with nervous, fearsome energy. She cannot ride; she will not do this. Her arms tighten across her chest as she shrinks back. But suddenly her father reaches down, sweeps her up into his arms and they ride away. Slowly at first, a gentle gallop, as the girl clings to her father in terror until she begins to realize that with him she is safe. How could she ever have thought otherwise? Soon, it seems, they are riding like she never imagined—the wind kissing her cheeks, her heart pounding in her chest, her eyes catching the world go past in a blur. Suddenly this is not terror, but unbelievable delight. This is life. This is just the beginning. Who knows what will come, or where it will end?

In Christ we have the promise that life is where it will end. Life is our possession and our direction. Sin, death, and the evil one will reach back into our lives again and try to rob us of life. At times the battles will be ferocious. At other times we may be scarcely aware that heaven and hell are doing battle in our lives. In either case we are summoned to remember our baptism: that we died with Christ, we rose with Christ, and even now we live with Christ. Where Christ is, there is life—and we are with him.

This companionship has come through the fires of hell itself. We are with Christ. To experience his presence is like water to parched lips. It is as uplifting as St. Patrick's prayer:

Christ be with me, Christ within me,
Christ behind me, Christ before me,
Christ beside me, Christ to win me,
Christ to comfort and restore me,
Christ beneath me, Christ above me,
Christ in quiet, Christ in danger,
Christ in hearts of all that love me,
Christ in mouth of friend and stranger.
I bind unto myself the Name,
the strong Name of the Trinity,
by invocation of the same,
the Three in One, and One in Three.[9]

Reflections on the water:

> *he dared to glance back*
>
> *and noticed from squinting eyes*
>
> *he was not there*

4. Always a Gift

Consider this scenario: A couple, the wife carrying a baby dressed in pink, walk into the pastor's study. The pastor didn't recognize them, but he welcomed them. "We've come to get our baby baptized," she said, right to the heart of the matter. For the next few moments they began to get acquainted, the pastor and these new parents who glowed with affection for their daughter. They hadn't met before, the husband said, because they didn't believe in church and so they didn't come to worship. They had been confirmed in the church and they lived in the area; their parents did, too. This was the first grandchild on either side of the family; the baptism was going to be "one really big deal," the very words of the baby's father. "So when can we get it done?"

In that moment the pastor knew that he and these young parents were looking at baptism with very different eyes. The pastor began to explain the meaning of baptism, that, from the earliest days of the Church, believing parents had brought their children for baptism, so that they could share the life of faith with them. Finally he said, "Before we make plans for your daughter's baptism, let's talk about your own faith as parents and how you will be practicing that."

The husband realized that this was going down a road he didn't want to travel. He held up his hand and said, "No, you don't understand. We don't want to talk about religion. We just want to get our daughter done. In fact, it's our right."

Did the pastor give in and baptize, even though this was troubling to him? Did the parents get angry and storm out, threatening to take steps involving other people, either family members or parish leaders?

This sort of conversation occurs in the church, including the Lutheran church. The Lutheran heritage goes back to state church beginnings in Europe, where baptism has often been understood and practiced as a right of the individual, rather like citizenship as a birthright. This practice migrated to America along with the European immigrants. For example, baptism was virtually automatic for a citizen of Norway who was also a member of the state church (Lutheran). Citizenship plus nearly universal membership in the church assumed the practice of the faith. In this situation baptism became individualistic, a formal and dignified naming ceremony. It was the child's right, claimed by the family.

That is why the father in our story said, "It's our right," and that is also why he is wrong. Baptism is never a right. It isn't something we can claim for ourselves over against the community of faith or church. It is not automatically ours like, for example, the civil right of voting privileges at a given age. We cannot claim it on some personal basis, such as our own baptism in the church or our family's history in a congregation.

Baptism is a gift of the Lord Jesus Christ himself, entrusted to the church as an instrument of the Gospel. Jesus has the authority over baptism and he authorized the community of faith, the church, to offer baptism as a way to make disciples. He said to his disciples, the first generation of that faith community, "Go therefore and make disciples of all nations, baptizing them . . ." (Matt. 28:19). Baptism and making disciples go together, and the church has the responsibility to use the sacrament in this way.

What's wrong with parents wanting baptism for their child? Nothing. Absolutely nothing. In fact, every pastor is delighted when parents want this. Wanting baptism, however, while not wanting the life of the baptized is the problem. Wanting the rite of baptism without interest in learning what it means is the problem. "Getting the child done," as the language of some puts it, without commitment to teaching the child faith in Jesus Christ, is the issue at stake. Why is this so? Because baptism is not merely a one-time act; it is the beginning of critical relationships, the key one with Jesus himself, but openness and availability to other members of the community of faith as well.

Dietrich Bonhoeffer, a Christian pastor and teacher, was a martyr for Jesus Christ in Germany close to the end of World War II. In a book about following Jesus, *The Cost of Discipleship*, he argued that the church was often guilty of dispensing "cheap grace." One of his examples was "baptism without church discipline," by which he meant offering the sacrament as a product.[10] Baptism is not a product or a mere ritual; it is a call to confess our sin, our need of God, and the inclination to act as our own ultimate authority. Coming to the church for baptism involves that humble confession.

This is where baptism gets exciting. If you come to the church to arrange baptism for your child and the pastor says, "Let's talk about Jesus and faith," instead of casually saying, "Okay, when do we schedule the baptism?" you are fortunate. By moving the conversation in this direction, the pastor gives you the opportunity to meet God. That's right. If you allow your pastor to be a spiritual guide, you have the possibility of experiencing God and the truth that really matters for your life.

In fact, you will be living in the grace and power of your own baptism if you give up your supposed "right" to have your child baptized, and instead open yourself to spiritual growth and understanding. Living in the grace and power of your own baptism means that you confess that Jesus is Lord of your life, not you. Letting go of your "right" to baptism is permitting your Lord to work on your heart in a new way.

We live in a time when many do not want to be religious, even though they are open to spirituality. Discovering that baptism is a divine gift—albeit a gift with great consequences—rather than a human right is a significant spiritual gift. Insistence that baptism is a human "right" often leaves the participants untouched and unchanged. Those who open their hearts to baptism as a gift of God—costly, wonderful, and inviting their response—experience the mysterious touch of the Spirit of God.

Reflections on the water:
> *the face lined with discontent*
> *the weight of all he didn't have*
> *undone by a gift*

"As the scripture has said, 'Out of the believer's heart shall flow rivers of living water.'"

John 7:38b

5. God Gets Physical

In the late spring of 2006 an eagerly awaited movie resulted in headlines focused on spiritual matters. Dan Brown's book, *The Da Vinci Code*, enjoyed a second spurt of publicity with the production and appearance of the movie. At the same time there was a lot of discussion of the "truth" of the story.

On the one hand, many readers took the book to be straightforward truth, biblical and historical truth, too. On the other hand, respectable scholars pointed out old fallacies in the story that had long since been discredited.

In the course of this controversy, the *Gospel of Judas* was published and offered as a discovery that would shake up biblical scholarship. This gospel was a latecomer to the early Christian scene, however, probably, in its earliest form, a hundred years after the biblical gospels. The current manuscript was discovered in Egypt. It dates to about A. D. 300. The text presents a form of Gnostic Christianity, considered a heresy by what later prevailed as orthodox Christianity. Interestingly, Dan Brown's characters in *The Da Vinci Code* exhibit similar Gnostic tendencies.

Gnosticism devalues the physical world. The name comes from the Greek word for knowledge, since those who held this viewpoint were on a quest for the secret knowledge that would lead to salvation. They disdained the physical on the ground that it was just the shell for what is hidden and real. That's why, in the *Gospel of Judas*, Jesus tells Judas that he will be greater than the other disciples, because he will "sacrifice the man that clothes me."[11] The physical world, including the human body, has little or no value for Gnostics. This has major implications for truth itself.

In baptism God gets physical. God uses water. He uses one part of the physical creation as a means to bring about a new creation. Though God transcends the world, he uses earth's elements to serve his purposes. They are both good and serve for good. When God washes ordinary water over a physical body, he affirms the value of the water and the body. He does not despise or reject them.

There is beauty and grace here. God the Father of Jesus is the same God who created all things and called each of them good. Human beings sometimes fret over whether they are spiritual enough. Baptism signifies, however, that God loves all of creation, that is, you and me and all that surrounds us. When we experience life in a body that works and plays, sweats and aches, grows stronger or loses muscle, then we are spiritual enough. That is, we are spiritual enough to know God's gift of real life. Baptism is real-world action for real-world people, not for people that we imagine we need to be.

Some churches have begun to practice baptism in a way that reflects a new appreciation of the physical. Though the amount of water used does not determine the validity of baptism, we are finding ways to use as much water as possible. We are not embarrassed by the physical, nor worried about spilling water liberally. In the spirit of Luther himself, a growing number of congregations are adding an immersion font for baptism. This very visible font not only becomes the dramatic setting of our dying to sin and rising to new life in Christ – the very heart of the sacrament – but it also becomes creation-affirming in the abundance of water.

A few years ago I heard with delight about a pastor who baptized a pre-school child with generous amounts of water, while she provided ongoing commentary. It went something like this: "In the name of the Father ("That's a lot of water") and of the Son ("And now he's getting it on me") and of the Holy Spirit ("And now my new dress is all wet"). Amen. Indeed. Amen to the action of a wonderful God who delights in creation and brings new life to creation in the sacrament.

Recently, when we were encouraging confirmands to ask questions, one of them surprised me. "Is baptismal water holy?" she wanted to know. I tried to assure her that it is not a magical kind of holy, something we can store in a jar for later supernatural effect. Still, baptismal water is water set apart for unique and extraordinary use through Jesus Christ. For that reason we don't treat it lightly. We might keep it in the font for a time, to touch and be reminded of the baptism. Then we pour it over the grass or a shrub while praising God both for creation and for new creation.

In the end it would be good to say a prayer of thanks for all water, a gift of God's creation and love. Water blesses our lives in more ways than we can number. Why be a Gnostic in such a world, as though we could be more spiritual than God?

Reflections on the water:

he looked for the spiritual

so very hard that the water

ran right off him

6. Dress Rehearsal

"Men hate to dress up; dressing up is really a woman's thing." I once used that line in a sermon at a wedding, an occasion when everyone had made some effort to look good, and the wedding party was standing before me resplendent in their dresses and tuxedoes. If you believe that line, I went on to say, how do you explain the hundreds of thousands of Wisconsin hunters who dress up as orange as pumpkins to hunt deer for nine days in November? The truth is that dressing up has many variations. We dress up to celebrate events for people we love, but, more than that, dressing up helps us to become what we need to be. Dressing up for a wedding, for example, puts us in the spirit of celebration. Dressing for deer hunting makes the woods safer for all hunters.

Our baptismal dressing up prepares us for the baptized life. The white gown is a sign that we have died to sin and now live the new life in Christ. It announces that this is who we are, Christians with a new identity in Christ. We are children of God, members of the community of faith.

We need to take this another step. This community into which we are baptized is a critical part of our future. Our dress-up entry into the church begins a lifetime of formation by the baptismal character of the church's life, especially its worship. We need the church and its worship to become the person God made us in baptism. This community is part of the gift, and worship in the sanctuary is the dress rehearsal for the baptismal spirituality that is our vocation in the world. The alb itself worn by the pastor – and often acolytes, assisting ministers, and choir – is actually an old baptismal garment. It is a visible sign of what we are and what we are becoming.

Let me say it again. Worship is a dress rehearsal for living the baptized life. Many Christians talk about worship as recharging time, rather like a spiritual gas station. What happens in worship is deeper. Worship shapes our spiritual lives. We say the words and practice the lines; we act out our new roles; we rehearse who we are and what we do. And we do all this with the sights, sounds, scents, and touch that prepare us to live in the world.

As we begin worship, we hear the words of invoking the Triune God and, with them, make the sign of the cross.[12] We do this in remembrance of our baptism. If, with all the "hats" we wear in the world, we have forgotten the greatest one of all, that we are children of God, the sign of the cross draws us into God's eternal love and truth. We are always "more" in Christ.

"If we say that we have no sin...." We begin with confession and forgiveness: these drive us to the heart of baptismal spirituality. We return to baptismal waters to die once more to our sin and emerge to new life. In these moments we acknowledge our wrongs individually, but also our wrongs as members of the human family. I find that I need a moment for quiet reflection at this point in worship; we must not move too quickly. To my disappointment, I have repeated my sins. If I am to rise up, it is only in Christ who forgives me once more, not because I have won the battle against sin. Jesus' love amazes me more each day.

Then comes the Word, that is, Scripture, sermon and, finally, the Creed, when I respond to the God who speaks as my God. In baptism we received everything that belongs to Christ. Moving through this worship sequence of Scripture, sermon and confession of faith, I experience once again the rich inheritance I have received from Christ in baptism. The words aren't just out there floating unattached in spiritual space. They have become personal words, like the sacramental words with bread and wine. This is "for you." It is indeed for you and me.

Now we come to the declaration of peace, the offering, and the prayers, ways we can live anew in the new creation of Christ. Peace takes shape physically as we extend our hand to others. If we are by nature shy, we may struggle with this gesture, but God is working with our enthusiasm or without. God's new world is coming. The offering invites us into the work of God, what we do to fulfill God's purposes as we go out into the world. The prayers are the words of our hearts, yearning for God's new creation. In thought, word, and deed, God shapes us through the liturgy.

In the bread and wine of the common meal Christ feeds us, reminding us that "One does not live by bread alone, but by every word that comes from the mouth of God" (Matt. 4:4). We do not live alone, but with God, and in the company of God's people. Gathered here, with all our flaws and differences, together we become the sign of what God is doing in Christ. We are not mere spectators. We are participants, acting our roles in the incredible drama that God will bring to completion.

We depart from worship, sent into the world in peace and for service.

In this time set apart for worship we rehearse, together with sisters and brothers in Christ, the role in life that we entered at our baptism. Worship shapes our lives to live the baptized life in a world that prefers to mold us in its image, with its values. Worship is our dress rehearsal, a time to experience in our bones what it is to belong to Christ and to be conformed to him (Rom. 12:1-2).

A couple chooses beautiful clothing for their wedding to celebrate this festive event. Deer hunters wear orange for safety and to signal the camaraderie of the season. Dressing up does things to us. The white gown of baptism signals that we are new, forgiven and free in Christ. Thereafter we need the regular dress rehearsal of worship to shape us for the life we entered when we dove into the deep baptismal waters.

Reflections on the water:
> *dressed to look the part*
> *her clothes sagged and bagged and dragged*
> *until she became them*

7. Safe in the Waters

"I don't want to die!" If I haven't spoken those words aloud, I've thought them. How about you? Sometimes we even scream them, seeking to defy a reality more terrible than we can bear.

The forty days of Lent are the church's experience of learning to die. Drawn into the life of Jesus and toward his suffering and death, we come face to face with our own dying. The passion hymn, "Go to Dark Gethsemane," includes a prayer that we may "learn from Jesus Christ to die."

The storm-tossed waters of a lake can remind us that we are never very far from dying. As a non-swimmer, I have trembled even in water embarrassingly shallow. The baptismal liturgy draws upon that life-and-death imagery to declare that in baptism we die and rise with Christ (see Rom. 6:3-4). The apprehension about physical death provides us a vivid metaphor for baptism. We need to explore the meaning of dying and rising with Christ in baptism.

Let's try it this way. If we take God's promise at face value, that we died in those baptismal waters and miraculously rose to new life, then, in a very real sense, our death is behind us. Death is an event of our past. Usually we view death as a threat of the future. We will die one day, yes we will, whether we like it or not, whether we prepare for it or not, death will get us. But Jesus reverses that thinking, saying to us, "because you have died and risen with me, life is what you have before you. You have life now, full and abundant life, even eternal life, life forever."

How dramatically real this becomes if our baptism takes place in an immersion font – a growing practice. Our baptism is valid regardless of the amount of water, that is true, but how boldly expressed it is when we are plunged into the font's deep water with Christ and we come up sputtering and gasping the air as his new creation!

I like the sound of that. Don't you? We want to live, really live. We don't want death doing its nasty number on us. If Jesus can do for us what we cannot do for ourselves, defeat death, we need to pay attention.

Take this another step. If death is behind me rather than ahead, Jesus has made it so. He has made my future secure and full of life. My destiny is tied to the only one who has risen from the dead. In fact, as St. Paul wrote, "you have died, and your life is hidden with Christ in God" (Col. 3:3).

One more step. If my life is "hidden with Christ in God," my life is secure. Death does not have the power to snatch us from God. In the earliest exposition on baptism in the church (ca. 200), the church father Tertullian wrote that Christians are like little fish, "safe in the waters" of our baptism.[13] We are safe because God connected us to the risen Christ in those waters to give us life.

The effect of this is powerful. We can learn how to die. That is, Christians can look at death with the confidence that it doesn't own us. This realization has the power to free us. In the 1940s German pastor and teacher Dietrich Bonhoeffer found himself in increasingly grave danger as he tried to live faithfully to Christ in Nazi Germany. Instead of acting out of fear, he decided—and this is my paraphrase—that faithful people don't ask how they are going to save their own skin, but, rather, how the next generation is going to live.[14] With death already behind him, Bonhoeffer lived boldly and confidently. Though he die physically, in Christ he would still be alive. On April 9, 1945, on a Nazi gallows, he declared, "For me this is not the end, but the beginning."[15]

I recall a young woman who struggled courageously with cancer for three years. The battle was an emotional roller coaster, but she kept living. Finally, death grabbed her and wouldn't let go. With tears, she and her family told stories and shared the intimacies of love. They filled their house with the laughter that baffles death and the devil. "What would we do without faith!" she said to me. I didn't have to answer, because it was not a question. She was living and she was also learning to die. She could do both, because, held by God in the embrace of Christ, she was "safe in the waters" of her baptism.

Learning to die has many dimensions. There is coming to terms with the will of God, and there is sacrifice. There is letting go, and there is change. We need to think about all of these things. We may shout, "I don't want this. I don't want to die." But Jesus Christ will teach us how to die.

He will lead us back to the font and remind us, "Remember how I held you and brought you through these waters from death to life. Learn from me." In the end we may arrive at the calm of Bonhoeffer or the confidence of the young woman with cancer, or we may be neither calm nor confident. What will matter is that we have Christ with whom we are "safe in the waters."

Reflections on the water:

> *face up in the water*
> *floating, it seemed,*
> *was like dying*

8. New Every Day

The baptized life is like the renewal that comes from a drenching rain after a bike ride on a very hot day. You feel alive again! The worn and aching body, the sun-dried skin, the bruised knees, the depleted spirit—all beg for an ending. Then raindrops tease with hope, until the heavens pour out their mercies. The rain refreshes and restores. Laughter and shouts fill the air. We are new persons, and wheels become wings. Body and spirit agree, this is life.

The heart of baptismal spirituality is like that. We meet it as confession and absolution, or confession and forgiveness. The preparation that begins our worship invites us to come before God mindful of our sins, "things we have done and things we have failed to do." Then the pastor declares "the entire forgiveness of all your sins, in the Name of the Father, and of the Son, and of the Holy Spirit. Amen."[16]

What happened? You have heard this announcement before. It may have become so routine that you didn't attend to it all that closely this time. It is nonetheless revolutionary. The pastor has declared you dead to sin and alive to Christ. Your sins are gone, dead, and you are a new person, alive. No matter how you feel, you need this gift, and it is yours.

Confession and forgiveness are familiar—no surprises here. The announcement often reaches distracted ears. Yet, even when our "lights are on and no one's home," God is at work on us. Step back for a moment and consider how wonderful this baptismal reality is: the dying to sin and rising to new life of our baptism happens over and over again. The hurts and wrongs of yesterday, the alienation from family and friends—all that is dead and gone. You get a fresh start. God knows that you need it. The announcement of absolution grants it. "If we confess our sins, he who is faithful and just will forgive us our sins" (I John 1:9). However familiar, however undeserved, it offers a new beginning each time.

So there we are, washed clean and made new, forgiven in spite of ourselves. This belongs to all of life, not simply to the hour of worship. A pastor friend, when asked to do a baptism at the child's home, hesitated, because baptism belongs within a community of believers. "Where should we do the baptism? In the washing machine?" he inquired.

The appeal of his brassy suggestion was that it connected the washing of baptism with ordinary life and made it lively in a physical, bodily way. We don't forget things that happen to our bodies. Sense experience—touch, smell, sight, even hearing—stamps the memory in the mind. When confession and forgiveness touch our whole body, their water-fresh and physical reality comes home to stay.

So, let me make a suggestion. Since confession and forgiveness are not matters of Sunday worship alone—though we need that regular assurance in the midst of the company of believers—find a way to experience these gifts every day. Take time for deliberate prayer, confessing to God the failings that burden your heart, especially those you find difficult to own. Be bold! You won't surprise God. Admit them and ask God to wipe your slate clean. Then go to the bathroom sink, fill it with water, scoop up water in your hands and splash it on your face several times, while praying, "God, I have sinned. Wash me clean." Enjoy the cleansing feel of the water. Then say, "I am forgiven and new. Thank you, God."

Ritual acts like this help us experience the reality of our life in Christ. Forgiveness is there without the ritual, but the physical act helps to make it "for you."

When a particular sin refuses to loose its grip on the soul, the church has another gift that we should use more frequently, the private confessional. The pain is deep when we have hurt others, and deeper yet, when they won't forgive us. The pain is deep when we know our guilt and are locked into its lonely cell. How persistent is the power of those sins for which we pray even every day. For such times God has given us pastors, to hear the confession of that which keeps us from experiencing the love of God and the fullness of life. After a confidential, honest sharing from the heart, the pastor places hands on our head, declares God's forgiveness, and prays for the comfort of the Holy Spirit. The physical touch of hands emboldens our trust that God's goodness is for us. At the same time, the pastor adds the assuring words that this is most certainly true.

The recurring theme is a return to our baptism. At every time of confession and forgiveness we experience once more the watery drowning and rising of baptism, when Jesus Christ bonded his destiny to ours. In Christ our sins lie dead and buried, washed away. Christ makes us new each day.

Reflections on the water:

the nasty cut of the paper

the sharp word to the heart both

need the mouth for healing

9. God Slept Here

With a group on an historical tour, you peer into a roped-off room and read the sign, "Abraham Lincoln slept here." You'd like to reach in and touch the quilt on the bed, despite the prohibition. Seeing and hearing bring reality close, but touching and feeling really bring it home. If we could sneak into that room and lie on Lincoln's bed, that would be even better.

The reminder that someone important was once here where I am now evokes a response in me. First something happened, perhaps long ago, and now I am responding to what happened. Baptismal spirituality is like that; it is response spirituality. God is what happened first, as "In the beginning ... God" (Gen. 1:1), or "In the beginning was the Word, and the Word was with God, and the Word was God" (John 1:1). Long before me, God was, and my life is a response to God. One day you were baptized "in the name of the Father, and of the Son, and of the Holy Spirit." God came to you and claimed you. As a consequence, your life, your whole life, is a response to God. First God acts, then we respond.

The world wants to reverse the order of spirituality. We come first, and then we try to figure out God. Take a look at the long shelves devoted to spirituality in our bookstores. Spirituality is a smorgasbord of everything imaginable, from Wicca witches to magic and crystals. As a people, we are hungry and curious. We search for that "something more" that will fill our emptiness. In the midst of the search, however, something else occurs. We conclude that we can put together a spirituality that suits our own tastes. A bit of this and a bit of that, and we'll have what we need for our emptiness. Our very own creation! Spiritual truth made just for us. It sounds good. The problem is that it is all made up.

Deep within, in the recesses of our soul, we know that it is a lie.

Sometimes our invented spirituality is simple—just a few clichés we've picked up along the way to keep the true God from messing with us. "I keep the Ten Commandments; that's my religion." "I don't go to church, because it's filled with hypocrites." "Jesus was a good teacher, but who can believe those miracles?" We put together our own package of truth, which offers no challenge to our assumptions and prevents us from encountering God.

God is at the center of baptismal spirituality, where God has always been. I have not arranged this world, including the religious or spiritual world. In baptism, God was here first and we believe. However long ago our own baptism, God chose to act upon us in water and Word. In the earthy, physical water that we see and that touches us, and in the Word that we hear, God named us his own with believers looking on and saying, "Yes." God gave us everything that belongs to Jesus and sealed it with the Spirit forever. From that moment on, our life is a response to God, as are the lives of our parents, our family, our godparents and the whole gathered congregation.

In baptism God is in your life and mine early on, before we have had a thought of God, much less a doubt. How will we respond? In baptism God joins us to Jesus Christ, who died on a cross for us and rose to life, that we might have genuine life ourselves. How will that make a difference in us? In baptism, the Holy Spirit gives gifts that come with Jesus: love, joy, peace, patience, kindness and more. How will we use them?

This spirituality is not just about me, especially not about me front, center, and always the focus. When we trust and live as though God has really acted in this humble event of water and the Word, God is really God in our lives, working in us to shape the promise.

If you are struggling with your response right now, that is okay. Wrestling with God is a common theme of Christian life. Believing is not an easy matter, but it is basic to life. Soren Kierkegaard, a Danish theologian/philosopher of the 19th century, suggested that becoming a Christian required a "leap of faith," that we had to take that leap even without fully compelling evidence. On the other hand, C. S. Lewis, the Englishman of "Narnia" fame, took a different point of view. He argued that we could make inferences from the available evidence, so that a "leap" was not necessary to arrive at faith. Whichever alternative you prefer, it is important to remember that both are responses to God's initiative. God comes to you first.

If you have been baptized, go back to that objective, historic moment in time and remind yourself, "I have been baptized." Say to yourself, "God was there, present for me. A God much greater than I or than my thoughts was there. This God acted to give me life." No matter what the level of your belief then, God continues to call to you in your baptism. Trust God now.

In *The Cost of Discipleship* Dietrich Bonhoeffer wrote that belief is not as difficult as we sometimes make it to be. We are all capable of taking "the first step" to worship God in the congregation where God promises to be present, present for us in the Word, in the bread and wine of the Eucharist, in the gathered people.[17] When we do this, we step once more into the baptismal waters and recognize God as the center of our lives.

Reflections on the water:

> *I Was Here First:*
>
> *her game pronouncement*
>
> *to the whole world*

10. What the Waters Reveal

Water is a powerful force. The terrible destruction of Hurricane Katrina in New Orleans and the surrounding country revealed that force on a massive scale. For example, the storm destroyed ninety per cent of the homes in nearby Harrison, casting their residents adrift in uncertainty.

Weeks after the hurricane, a magazine published a feature article with the title, "What the Waters Revealed."[18] Everyone knew what the waters covered and hid; those scenes appeared repeatedly in the news media. This article displayed what America had overlooked: the depth of human poverty in this unique American city. The waters were truth-telling waters. Right in the heart of one of our great cities, people lived in conditions that we either had not noticed or simply avoided. The waters of Hurricane Katrina were destructive, but at the same time they were revealing. They made it difficult to ignore the depth of poverty in the lives of fellow Americans.

That water reveals should be no surprise to Christians, that it uncovers through its washing what is foundational and true. That is what happens in our baptism. Baptism "in the name of the Father, and of the Son, and of the Holy Spirit" bonds our lives to the One "who is, and who was, and who is to come" (Rev. 1:4). It centers and anchors our lives in the Lord of the universe. All other truths are dependent on that and secondary to it.

Baptism is the power of God for blessing us with a capacity for truth. That power is present in one of the simplest and most direct of symbols, the washing of water. As the pastor washes water over the head of the baptized—or pours it more generously in other practices—water does what it ordinarily does every day of our lives. It washes us clean. In the traditional language of baptismal theology, God uses water to cleanse us of original sin.

Consider this example. Your ten-year-old son, while riding his bike, takes a terrible spill on the road. He rushes into the house crying and holding his hand, a mess of mud and blood, dirty grass and gravel. You run to his side. It is impossible to see the wound clearly, so filled with road residue. You just know that he needs help and that you need to see the wound. You rush him to the sink to wash the hand. Even as he whimpers in pain, you continue the washing. For the water reveals what you need to know.

Even then, the wound is only part of the truth. The greater truth is that the hand will heal, given time. So it is with our lives in a larger sense. Our sin is not the final truth. It does not have the last word. God does—the Father, Son, and Holy Spirit into whom we are baptized. The waters of baptism help us see both our need and the promise of life in God.

On our own we want to see the world on our terms, as our world, in our way, to our advantage. That is the way of the old Adam, the way of nature that runs through the entire history of humankind. The return to baptism rescues us from this empty self-centeredness. In that return we repent, turn around and walk a new direction. We return to live in the waters of our baptism, wash away the grime of our wounded lives and find healing in God.

Joe discovered how this worked for him. He was a successful young man. Within a few years following college graduation, he was earning more than his father earned at the end of a long career. He thought he could have everything and experience everything. The only problem was that, every time he added a new thrill or an expensive toy, the satisfaction didn't last.

Joe began to doubt that his dedication to material success held the meaning of life. He thought about the really happy people he knew, and how many of them didn't seem to need what he was chasing. He asked some of them about their choices in life and discovered a couple surprises. Many of them measured their success by what they gave to others, and many of them were Christians. Joe sensed his dissatisfaction with much in his own life, and he confessed that unease to God. He even found his way back to his home church, wrestling with himself every mile of the way.

On that particular day the pastor invited worshippers to place their fingers in the waters of the baptismal font, touch the water to their brows, and say quietly to themselves, "I am a beloved child of God." Even Joe did this. He felt the touch of the water gently cooling the fever of his emptiness and giving him a sense of being close to truth. He hadn't experienced anything like this in a long time. He didn't know where it would lead, but he caught a glimpse of a different sort of life. It felt good, very good.

Joe didn't need to return to the baptismal font of his home church in his quest for a better life. God works in various ways to grant us a vision of genuine life. Yet, there at the font we are face to face with what the waters of baptism reveal: the poverty of life on our own and the riches of God's love. The baptismal waters run deep.

Reflections on the water:

she watched the water

recede in the glass as she drank

and she was still thirsty

"As a deer longs for flowing streams,
so my soul longs for you, O God."

Psalm 42:1

11. Sleeping and Waking

Hardly anything we do is as ordinary as falling asleep and waking up. Only after thinking again about Martin Luther's Morning and Evening Prayers did it occur to me that these ordinary experiences help us to understand baptismal spirituality. They are a metaphor for living the baptized life, and they are more: sleeping and waking in themselves can be living the faith into which we were baptized.

Imagine this night for yourself. Your day has gone well, but in the evening a call from your daughter changes everything. You welcome her phone calls, but tonight you sense immediately that something is very wrong. There is none of the usual teasing laughter in her voice, and before you inquire what is amiss she bursts out, "And now he wants out of our marriage!" Stunned at those words, you grab for something to hold to. You need to sit down. "Oh, sweetie, no, no!" You spend the next hour listening and crying. In shock, you cannot believe it. Never, ever did you see this coming.

Two hours later it is time for bed. You have listened and talked, cried and talked some more, first with your daughter herself, then with your husband. Amidst the tears and words your very sighs become prayers to God, questions to God, pleas to God. What is going on here, God? What?

As you pull the blanket over yourself, you realize that sleep will not come easily tonight. Five-thirty comes quickly, however, and you need to try. Again you pray, oh do you pray, until words fail and your mind is numb. How could this happen to your own dear daughter, and your son-in-law? You had no clue. But were there clues? Scenes race through your mind. You remember sharp words between them. Was there more you should have seen, but missed? What do you do now? If you had a suggestion, would anyone listen?

Images race through your mind like scenes cut from a movie, none of them pleasant. And sleep? Who can sleep when the world needs fixing?

Martin Luther faced a similar question when his world was in turmoil. The pressures of religious controversy confronted him on all sides: the church as it had been was collapsing, and Luther lived in the shadow of threats to his life. Incredibly, he didn't crack under the pressure. Rather, in the midst of this confusion, he wrote an Evening Prayer which expresses a firm trust in the goodness of God:

We give you thanks, heavenly Father, through Jesus Christ your dear Son, that you have graciously protected us today. We ask you to forgive us all our sins, where we have done wrong, and graciously to protect us tonight. Into your hands we commend ourselves: our bodies, our souls, and all that is ours. Let your holy angels be with us, so that the wicked foe may have no power over us. Amen.[19]

After this prayer the Christian may simply lie down and sleep. This is an expression of faith, the confidence that God will hold us in his arms and bear in his heart the problems for which we see no solution. God gives us this gift of peace through the night and strength for the coming day.

What better gift in the depths of a troubled night? In our heart of hearts we know that we cannot make things right at 3:00 a.m. Where this is going is unclear, this shocking mess beyond our control, but worry will not fix it. We know that, and God knows that. So God invites us, even commands us, to lie down and sleep. God will continue working while we sleep; that's a promise. The command is to release our worries, our tossing and turning, trusting that God wills us to sleep.

Falling asleep is a form of dying. Letting go into the unconsciousness of sleep imitates the letting go of dying and resting in the arms of God. When we fall asleep, we do not know the outcome. We could die, or we could rise refreshed.

We do not know. Falling asleep is an expression of trust in God, a God who holds us in tender, powerful arms no matter what the outcome of the night.

Our childhood prayer expresses this truth: "Now I lay me down to sleep; I pray the Lord my soul to keep. If I should die before I wake, I pray the Lord my soul to take." This prayer expresses trust in God that we are going to "wake" no matter what. We will either wake, splash water on our face, and mumble over a bowl of oatmeal at breakfast. Or we will awaken in God's bright eternal kingdom. God will be with us in both places. What deep water for the soul!

Try this tonight: as you get into bed and turn off the light, pray aloud to God that he grant you the trust that releases your worries and eases you into sleep, for this night first but for all life as well.

Lying down and going to sleep can be a spiritual practice of trust in God. Instead of worrying about the measure of our faith, permit the simplicity of getting into bed and falling asleep to demonstrate trust that God will give us what we cannot give ourselves: a new day, another beginning, hope, resurrection.

Reflections on the water:

eyes sprung wide open

staring into space for sleep

and for God

12. Looking Into the Darkness

Is it theatrics or truth? That is what I wonder as I think about a moment in the baptismal service, the presentation of a lighted candle to the newly baptized. I love to hear the words of Jesus, "Let your light so shine before others that they may see your good works and glorify your Father in heaven."[20] I thrill to see the candle lighted from the large paschal candle and then passed on to this new member of the Christian family. There is so much light—from the candles, in the faces of those circling the font, and throughout the room. Light everywhere! That causes me to wonder.

What if we switched off all the lights in the sanctuary at that moment, leaving only the lighted Christ/paschal candle? In the semi-darkness we see clearly the passing of the light from the Christ candle to the baptismal candle. Since darkness closes in on all sides in our world, around us and within us—sin, selfishness, greed, anger, revenge, violence, unbelief—the light of that candle signals the light of Christ's promise. It is ours in baptism, and no one can switch it off.

Theatrical, to be sure, but it proclaims the truth of baptism. I could imagine Martin Luther himself pointing out that as we look into the darkness there is Christ. However deep the darkness, seeping even into the soul, Christ is there for us. No matter what your darkness—the difficulty of believing, the losses that wrench your spirit, the gloom that refuses to lift—Christ shines for you. The Christ we see in the darkness is not a chance sighting. He is God's aim that overcomes the darkness, a beam straight from the heart of God.

From the earliest days of Christianity, light has been the sign of our Lord at work. The Apostle Paul, in his letter to the Ephesians, cites an early Christian hymn, "Sleeper, awake! Rise from the dead, and Christ will shine on you" (5:14). Light marks the presence of the power of Christ. Even though we are darkness, Christ calls us into his light to become light, and it begins with our baptism.

When we were baptized, the world glowed with light. The light, however, is not our own; it comes from the light of Christ, signified by the lighting of the baptismal candle from the Christ candle. It continues to glow by virtue of its source.

To sustain the light we have the Word. "Your word is a lamp to my feet and a light to my path" (Ps. 119:105). We have the word of Scripture, and at its center the Word that is Jesus Christ himself. "And the Word became flesh and lived among us" (John 1:14). To know the Word is to become light amidst the darkness of the world.

Light is our vocation from God: "In the same way, let your light shine before others, so that they may see your good works ... " (Matt. 5:16). Christ shines for us; we shine for others. Or better, Christ shines in us for others. Light is a symbol for every good work we do when Christ lives within us. Amazing things happen in ordinary lives because of Christ. I have witnessed these things, and the glow of such discipleship humbles me.

One such light was a man so ordinary he would have gone unnoticed anywhere. After 27 years of marriage, his wife developed multiple sclerosis. Fifteen years she lived with this crippling disease, completely bedridden in the last three of those years. He was her caregiver day and night. He read to her. He opened the windows so that she could hear the birds. He fed and bathed her, even when she became incontinent. In countless faithful ways he loved her. In the last months, when I stopped by to share Holy Communion with them, she could not move her head, only her mouth, lips, and eyes. At the last, only her eyes. He was there through it all, never making her feel that she was a burden. Every kind gesture shone with gentle light. To commend him was to embarrass him, for he had answered the call to discipleship and gladly accepted the duties of love.

People who are light in the darkness bless the world. Some attract wide attention—Mother Teresa in her care for the dying poor, Martin Luther King, Jr. for his passionate, non-violent resistance to racism, Tom Fox on a 2006 peace mission to Iraq fully aware of the dangers that cost him his life. The light of Christ shone in their lives with fierce intensity.

Bishop Fulton J. Sheen, a pioneer of religious broadcasting, always ended his programs with the words, "It is better to light one candle than to curse the darkness." He had it right. In Christ we have the true light that brightens the world. It comes to us in baptism, with or without the theatrics.

Reflections on the water:

distant light distinctly
suspended in the tripping darkness
speaking defiance

13. Making the Sign

The sign of the cross is a gift. A pastor made that sign on us in baptism, before we had even a fleeting thought of God. It can become a normal expression of our baptismal spirituality.

Many Christians wear a cross on a neck chain or on a jacket lapel, or mount a decorative cross on a wall at home. While these have their value as testimonies to faith, actually making the sign of the cross upon ourselves can have a deeper spiritual impact, on us and even on our world.

I suggest making the sign of the cross on our bodies as a ritual practice, preferably as a thoughtful habit. It works in the following way. With your right hand gently closed, use the tip of your thumb to touch, in sequence, your forehead, your breastbone, your left shoulder and right shoulder as you speak softly the words, "In the name of the Father, and of the Son, and of the Holy Spirit. Amen." Practice it several times. An alternative to the use of the thumb is to touch together your thumb, index, and middle fingers as a sign of the Trinity, and use them together to make the sign.

Practicing this sign will make it feel natural, eventually a normal and important part of your spiritual practice. For Christians the sign of the cross is a thing of beauty, the ugliest instrument of cruelty and death turned by God into a sign of life and salvation. St. Paul is right, that to the world its message is foolishness, but he is also correct that to those who "are being saved it is the power of God" (1 Cor. 1:18).

Rituals have a powerful and positive effect on us. They connect us to deep spiritual truths and abiding values. They have the further advantage of affecting our whole person. A cross you wear, for example, you may or may not notice. When you make the sign of the cross upon yourself, however, you involve your whole body: the touch of your fingers, the movement of your hand and arm, the sound of words, the sight of your action, perhaps even the scent of your hand as it moves past your face. It takes but a moment of time in a particular place for a significant impact, such as making it the first act of the day when you rise from sleep. Use it to remember your baptism at the beginning of worship, or sign yourself as part of a brief prayer before eating.

If this practice is new to you, as it once was to me, morning and evening prayers or personal devotions may be good occasions for beginning. From there you could move to a family or church setting. I am pleased, for example, to see the sign made more frequently at the beginning of public worship or at the reception of the Lord's Supper. One day you may even begin using it in the wider public world to which God sends us to work and to witness.

Why would you do this? My simple answer is: because you are a Christian. No ritual sign declares that more clearly to us and to the world. But allow me to explain at greater length three reasons for making the sign.

First, it reminds us who we are. We are children of God. He so loved us in Jesus Christ that he died for us and made us his own family. This is our identity. I have heard it said that it makes all the difference in our lives if there is one person in the world who is "crazy about us." Our lives are immeasurably better when we know that someone loves us unconditionally. And yet if we cannot identify such a person, God wants us to hear from him, "You are my beloved, worth living and dying for." In fact, on days when we need such reassurance, it is good to speak those words as words from God, after we make the sign of the cross.

Next, the sign of the cross reminds us to whom we belong, Jesus Christ himself, who made us his own by defeating sin, death, and the power of evil. "You are not your own; for you were bought with a price" (1 Cor. 6:20). Once masters marked slaves with a sign of ownership, just as ranchers brand cattle. Even soldiers bore a distinctive mark. It is love that makes the sign of the cross such good news. Jesus does not own us to use and abuse us. In him we belong to one who is the loving heart of the universe. No matter who wants a piece of us today, no matter that the world views us as a production unit in an economic machine, in Christ we are always more.

Finally, the sign of the cross reminds us of our vocation, discipleship in a family of disciples. As a sister or brother in this family, I represent the family. My thoughts, words, and deeds are those of a disciple who names Jesus Lord. All that belongs to Jesus comes to me as a member of his family. No longer will anyone say of me, simply, "That's Garven's child, looks just like his father." Now there is an identity that runs deeper and remains forever. I am Christ's, being formed in his likeness. The sign of the cross, conforming us to Christ, reminds us to examine our lives under the question: How can I be a faithful disciple.

The baptismal water quickly evaporates, but the sign of the cross remains. Water and the cross are boldly physical, and God uses them to reach us and transform us. God is not spiritually remote, but uses his own creation to touch our lives through simple signs like making the cross. The sign is not a sacrament in itself, but it is sacramental.

Reflections on the water:

stares burn into my back

as I sign the cross more deeply

this is who I am

14. Jesus Never Comes Alone

My younger sister was born when I was ten years old. I recall her baptism on a Sunday afternoon on the home farm in one of those Wisconsin valleys we call coulees. Why at home, I don't know. Perhaps she had been ill and Mother hesitated to take her out in a crowd. Still, there were a few people present. Baptism always involves a community of people. If the pastor had been the only one there, my sister would still have had the community with her, for the pastor would have been the window to the church, all the others with whom she was now connected. There is no baptism without a community.

I encourage families to celebrate baptism within a worship service at the church. A wide variety of people as participants best expresses the community dimension of the sacrament. It is a valid baptism with the child and pastor alone, but a proper setting and vivid symbols open us to the richness of what God is doing.

When I was a student at Luther Seminary, I recall Alvin Rogness, president of the seminary and beloved Lutheran pastor, saying, "When Jesus comes into your life, he never comes alone." How true! When Jesus comes into a life at baptism, a flood of people comes streaming in—all the Christians of the past, your own baptized family, the baptized in the congregation, those baptized into Christ in Ethiopia, and that is just the beginning. Baptism is never just a ceremony for one child. God includes the world in every baptism.

To be sure, the presence of certain people may be more important at a particular moment. Parents take on personal responsibility for this child. They owe that care, not only because the child is theirs, but also because they have themselves been baptized into Christ. The congregation that witnesses the baptism has a responsibility, too, to support the parents with discipling ministry, to surround them with prayer, and to even call them to account if necessary. That is why Dietrich Bonhoeffer describes the church's role in baptism as "carrying the child," acting as mother to the child of God. [21] Baptism is a call to come to faith in a caring community. The church is more than a place to learn about God. It is a special place where Christ lives in the gathered people, or, in Bonhoeffer's words, a place where "Christ exists as community."[22]

We typically underestimate the importance of the community. In my congregation grandparents sometimes bring grandchildren to worship. The parents may be working, or they may not understand the value of their spiritual care. Grandparents can be a powerful sign of a community that cares for the faith of the next generation. They are examples of faith to their grandchildren and an important part of the answer to the question whether the future church will have children.

When Jesus comes, however, he brings with him more than these people of obvious importance and blessing. In his ministry he welcomed children in ways that surprised adults. He related to women with the sort of respect that stunned men. He touched lepers when others kept their distance. He associated with those whom society classified as sinners. He lunched with one whose financial affairs were a scandal. When Jesus comes, he doesn't bring just "nice folks."

Jesus welcomes people to his table for his Supper. There he reminds them of the wideness of God's mercy and the expanding circles of kinfolk. In the sacrament we have a vision of a new world, Republicans and Democrats together, rich and poor, young and old. God surprises us with neighbors at the communion table. We would arrange the place cards more carefully; we would guard the status quo of our comfortable old world.

What a strange assortment of people Jesus places together at his table—neighbors who disputed a property line, young mothers who know that their children are superior and expect others to take notice, a family whose son has returned home with AIDS. There they all are, gathered before the altar. Jesus welcomed them with the water of baptism and joined their lives to ours, lives messy, hurting, and needy, just like yours and mine.

The water of baptism makes us one community in Christ. Thereafter God transforms us to the shape of Christ, painful at times, but often a delight. In Christ we are the "dazzling bouquet" of Bret Hesla's song. "Mine is the church where ev'rybody's welcome. I know it's true 'cause I got through the door. We are a dazzling bouquet of ev'ry kind of flower. Jump in the vase, 'cause we've space for more."[23]

Reflections on the water:

> *people moving in measured steps*
> *arranging their kneeling neighbors*
> *at what is not the Lord's Supper*

15. In the Name

Do we need someone to convince us that our name is important? Not likely. I recall an occasion when a teacher asked a classmate how to pronounce his name, Maurice, whether Morris or Maureece. He responded that either was fine, that it didn't matter. The class laughed, amazed. We recognized that we didn't view our own names as that malleable. Our names expressed our uniqueness.

One day, with the pouring of water on our heads, a pastor baptized us "in the name of the Father, and of the Son, and of the Holy Spirit." Baptism connected us with a unique God, the Father of Jesus of Nazareth, known to us in the power of the Spirit. Holy Trinity names this God, whose fullness, mystery, and majesty require such a name.

We ought to rejoice in this name. It is a strong guard against all attempts to tame God, to reduce God to what we consider more politically correct or more fitted to our personal experience. In other words, baptism in the name of this God grants us a far greater God than one we might create in our own image.

For this reason the baptism of infants makes good sense. The name of God comes as a pure gift to one who is utterly dependent. Infants are a blank slate with respect to God. God grants them in baptism the name that they will hear and speak with the familiarity of "Mama" and "Daddy."

This name belongs to a very specific, particular God. We live in an age when it is common to say that "we all believe in the same God" or "we're all going to the same place." In fact, challenging such statements counts as bad taste. The assumption is that anyone can invent a religion and describe a suitable God. Such an assumption well deserves its critics.

The God of our baptism has a specific name, gathers us into a specific community of faith, and stands revealed in specific Scriptures. This God has claimed us in the water of baptism and given us life in the Triune name.

Is that limitation frustrating, to be claimed by one God, when others around us encourage us to explore a world of possibilities? A bit of Buddhism, a few New Age crystals, Horatio Alger's self-help god for success, the latest pop preacher—all these beckon us as possibilities to try. We can learn valuable things from the world about us—curiosity is a gift of God—but dabbling in the latest fad produces more exhaustion than truth.

The God of your baptism offers a better alternative. Take the word of this God, learn in the Spirit to trust the Father of Jesus, forego other alternatives and live as a follower of the Son of God, Jesus. Does that sound like death, giving up all those other possibilities, including designing my own spirituality? It is a death. This death is in the water of baptism itself. We die to sin in that water and rise to new life. That is, we die to our self-determining religious impulses and our desire to be the center of our universe. We rise to new life with Jesus Christ, the living Lord of the Scriptures of the Christian community.

In baptism God grants us freedom that many in our age do not understand. They think of religion—more likely now named spirituality—as a smorgasbord from which one selects what appeals to taste and hunger. The illusion of satisfaction may endure for some time, but the hunger remains. Sometimes the disappointing truth shows through, that this human spiritual creation is, finally, the façade of a very empty place.

Baptism's wonderful freedom is the knowledge that God has chosen us, loved us, and died and risen for us—all to give us life in his specific name. As we learn to trust this God, at the cost of abandoning all other gods, we experience the joy and freedom of the new life this God promises. This living in the name is an experience of dying and rising. It is baptismal spirituality.

Reflections on the water:
> *Jesus of Nazareth*
> *the name above every name*
> *God is so particular*

16. The Rhythms of Prayer

Is there a prayer that flows more richly with the beauty and truth of baptismal spirituality than the following prayer attributed to St. Francis of Assisi? Notice the wave-like movements and the repetition that connect the one who prays with the heart and life of Christ himself. Pray it now.

Lord, make us instruments of your peace.
Where there is hatred, let us sow love;
where there is injury, pardon;
where there is discord, union;
where there is doubt, faith;
where there is despair, hope;
where there is darkness, light;
and where there is sadness, joy.
Grant that we may not so much seek
to be consoled as to console;
to be understood as to understand,
to be loved as to love;
for it is in giving that we receive,
it is in pardoning that we are pardoned,
and it is in dying that we are born to eternal life.[24]

This is a prayer we can return to repeatedly for the deepening of the baptized life. Like a wave's powerful tow, this prayer moves us into deeper waters that shape our character. Drawn from one challenge of the Christian life to another, we would be swamped, save for the peace of Christ.

Dive into the waters of baptismal spirituality here.

First we hear and feel the poetry, the rhythm of the seven lines beginning "where," then three "to be," and finally three more "it is in." Each line alone points a spiritual direction, a direction for which Christ himself is the pioneer. Yet each successive line adds to the fullness of Christ's life in us as it rolls to the next. We feel the sweep of the lines, gathering momentum as we pray them, especially as we pray aloud. We become a part of the movement; the rhythm draws us into the prayer and into Christ himself. As we pray, line-by-line, we sense a reality larger than we—someone, actually, Jesus Christ. The prayer draws us in and lifts our lives to the realm of hope. We feel, we know: our lives are taking on the contours of the life of Christ.

The rhythms are dramatic and tough, a movement of dying and rising, from beginning to end. Whether we forgive someone for a hurt or die at the end of our years, we abandon a part of us we'd love to keep. We may even love our grudges, for example. They provide us a temporary, though illusory power. We love life, too, enough that we're in no rush to leave. In Christ, however, we learn that life is richer when we can let go of ourselves and, in the free fall of faith or even in the darkness of doubt, cling to him.

Here is the heart of baptismal spirituality. To let go and reach out to Christ is neither so blind nor so chancy as we feared. In that heart-throbbing moment, we discover Christ already reaching out to us. Such times summon us to remember our baptism, that we have already died and that our lives are secure in Christ.

To remember the promise we have in Christ is vital. Jesus clearly says, "Unless a grain of wheat falls into the earth and dies, it remains just a single grain; but if it dies, it bears much fruit" (John 12:24). The metaphor makes it sound so natural, even easy. Simply die, and then bear fruit! Before we dismiss Jesus as out of touch, let us recall the witness of his life. This is he, who, the night before his death, prayed that the cup might pass from him. Abandoned even by his closest friends, he cried out to God in desperation from the cross. This dying was not easy; it was not natural. Yet it was true, full of truth, more than human sense could grasp. That is why the baptismal spirituality of St. Francis' prayer is so valuable. Its language and rhythms take us where we cannot go alone.

Finally, the prayer expresses the larger truth, that we live in this spirituality all of our lives. His examples comprehend all of life, making clear that we never become so spiritual or so mature that we no longer need to die. Injury continues to be a fact of our lives; doubt and sadness do not disappear. The prayer does not present an ascending spirituality, one form for childhood, another for the mature Christian. Wherever we are in our spiritual journey, the patterns of this prayer continue with us. There are ever new dyings and risings in our life in Christ. Children who need forgiveness for failing to share learn that lesson, but, in our acquisitive society, adults consumed with things have not yet reached maturity.

Once I read a phrase added within the last line of St. Francis' prayer: "it is in dying [to ourselves] that we are born to eternal life." The Scriptures support this clarification, that, when we die and rise in our daily lives, eternal life begins now. It may come to full expression on the date engraved on our tombstone, but we experience it every day. Every forgiven injury is a taste of eternal life, as is every beam of light lighting our darkness and every tear wiped away to make room for joy.

With St. Francis' prayer we live in the water and waves of our baptism, and we move along.

Reflections on the water:
> *breathing in, Lord have mercy*
> *breathing out, Christ have mercy*
> *it is good to come alive*

17. The Rite Gift

Where did the notion arise that rituals are meaningless? The first time I saw someone other than a pastor make the sign of the cross was at the free throw line in a basketball game. It seemed very strange to me, coming as I did from a parochial Lutheran background. Not even a successful shot would have changed that. However, it is finally necessary to lay aside trivial first impressions. Rituals, like the ordinary good habits of our daily lives, may serve us very well.

A pastor first made the sign of the cross on us at our baptism. Most Lutherans have rarely, if ever, used the sign since that time, even though they hear a pastor suggest, in the course of a worship service, "The sign of the cross may be made by all in remembrance of their Baptism."[25] The sign of the cross anchors us in the heart of our spiritual beginnings.

For many adults making the sign of the cross may be a new and strange experience. Don't let that deter you. The value and truth of the sign transcend discomfort. Further, we need to find ways to help children use and appreciate this ritual practice. Children love rituals, and we can encourage and shape their faith through such ritual actions as the sign of the cross.

One of my special joys as a pastor is to preside at the Lord's Supper, sharing Christ in the bread and wine with my congregation. People of all ages come forward to participate. The youngest children come forward with their families to receive a blessing. This blessing is the sign of the cross on their foreheads along with the words, "The love of the Lord Jesus be with you always."

Some children are looking aside, and I catch them unprepared. Occasionally a child resists the touch, and that is okay. But now and then, when I make the sign and speak the words, the child nods, as if to say, "Yes, Pastor, I know it is true." That is a blessing for me as well as for the child. The first time it happened, I thought I had better remember this moment, because I wouldn't see it again. However, it has happened several times. Each time I stand in awe of the power of God in the simple ritual act of signing.

Children love these rituals, the thoughtful repetitive actions (even habits) that include them in the faith life of the people of God. If they could give voice to their experience, others would not dismiss rituals as empty religious gestures, but rather embrace them as welcoming actions that children can depend on when they join in the worship of God. They need such gestures, just as adults value an embrace from someone who forgives them.

Rituals are deep water for the soul of the child. They nourish faith in ways that their simple presence in the sanctuary or the pastor's words alone cannot accomplish. This is due in part to the touch of the hand or finger in tracing the sign of the cross. This warm, caring, safe touch extends the welcome of baptism in yet another way and helps the child experience life in a Christ-centered community. These rituals can be as important as the experience of love and touch in our earliest development as children.

Our faith communities need to find ways to enrich the ritual experience of children as well as adults. One example is to keep the baptismal font open, to allow parents to dip their fingers into the water and gently touch their child's head. This helps us to remember whose we are. Adults and older children can trace the cross on their own.

Increasingly we are relearning in the church what we have already known: that parents and other key adults are critical to our children's faith development. We cannot pass this responsibility to the church in general or Sunday School or confirmation instruction. This is encouraging news for parents; it means that they play a key role.

Rituals in the home are important for faith formation, saying grace together at mealtimes or reading and prayers at bedtime, for example. Children learn from these times with their parents—and grandparents, too—that faith is as natural as the air we breathe.

Some families adopt the sign of the cross for use in the home. One father makes the sign of the cross on the forehead of each of his children as they go off to school in the morning. He adds these words of blessing: "You are a child of God. In the name of the Father, and of the Son (+), and of the Holy Spirit. Go in love and peace." In one family this ritual practice is so much a part of daily life that the children remind their dad to "do them" if he happens to forget.

Rituals run deep. They are powerful signs of love and belonging, blessing and identity. Indifferent attitudes and casual use can trivialize them. However, they offer the possibility of running the waters of faith deep within the lives of our children. They are a rite gift to pass on—and a right one too.

Reflections on the water:

feeling the damp cross

she remembered who she really was

even when she forgot

"They are like trees planted by streams of water,
which yield their fruit in its season,
and their leaves do not wither ... ."

Psalm 1:3

18. Real People

There I was again, praying my irritable prayer. "God, make the church more like me. Mrs. Johnson is fussing about Bible study again. Fred is uptight over money—our lack of it, actually—and bending everyone's ear. Mr. Conservative himself—you know who I mean—practically threw a fit as he critiqued my 'liberal' sermon. That was liberal? If he wants liberal, I could show him. What is wrong with these people? You made them; you fix them! Couldn't they be at least a little more like me—reasonable, thoughtful, slow to anger? Sorry, God, I admit that I'm not so slow just now. But you understand, don't you? Where in the world are these people coming from? You tell me. Amen."

Does this sound familiar? Have you ever been exasperated by this strange bunch around you in this group called the church? Upon reflection, I realized that the only way to avoid such people is to quit the church. That is what a lot of folks do. Give me that old time religion, God, but no people! Give me spirituality; give me heavenly, mountaintop, mind-expanding spiritual experiences, but no messy people. If that were possible, there would be no need for my embarrassing prayer. Just ignore others in their ignorance. I can do it, but it's a spiritual lie.

"Where in the world are these people coming from?" I admit that I don't really want an answer from God. However, if I stop talking and listen—that other part of prayer—then I may hear God saying: "They came from the font, from the same waters of baptism that washed you. And, by the way, have you noticed that you are not always so sweet-smelling yourself?" I may hear that, yes, I do hear that, when I listen. God loves real people—impatient, irritable, politically incorrect people—and very real.

The wide course of the water of baptism carries us into the heart of God's love for the world. God created this world, beautiful and battered as it is, and God is not abandoning the "project." In fact, "project" is the wrong term, because it ignores the personal nature of God's work. God is not a spiritual mechanic, but a lover of creation who walks and talks, cries and laughs, and even suffers and dies with us. God does this not to "fix" us, but in loving us to show us the glorious reality of life.

The love of "real" people is difficult. I recall a young man who organized an educational experience for the children of the congregation. He sought the right leaders and was delighted with a woman who volunteered. "She told me," he said with enthusiasm, "how much she loved children. That's just the kind of person we need." Days later I found him dejected and asked what had happened. "I discovered that, when she said she loved children, she meant her own children." Other children were too boisterous, too messy, too loud, too smelly. The problem of real people surfaced.

Occasionally, I receive a request to baptize a child at a time other than a worship service, at home perhaps, or at a more convenient time. Except in rare circumstances, I resist. Why? Because the fullness of baptism requires the presence of people. It will be a baptism with one, or two, or three, but the presence of the congregation makes the point that we join a people that God chooses, not we. Those people will include more variety, sizes, shapes, opinions, and convictions than we are comfortable with—which is exactly what God wants. The church is the body of Christ, the gathered community of Jesus, God's creation and not ours. We don't have to like it, but God calls us to love it as we love Jesus himself. That can be delightful; it can also be painful. But it's real, the only world in which God works.

Dietrich Bonhoeffer said that Christ apart from the congregation is unthinkable. He added that the pursuit of sanctification (read: spirituality) apart from the church is to declare ourselves holy on our own.[26] To grow, we need the church of real people to love. We need "those hypocrites" who know they need forgiveness—real people, all of them.

A pastor was intensely engaged in conversation with a woman, trying to convince her to give his church a try. "You wouldn't be asking me," she dared him, "if you really knew me." The pastor was persistent in his invitation. "Well, try this on for size, and then tell me if I am welcome. Every Wednesday night I commit adultery with a married man. I've tried to call it off, but I cannot. I keep going back to him, even though I know it is wrong. So, that's me. Is your invitation still open to me?"

A real person. How do you think that pastor answered her?

The e-mail came to me like a lightning strike on a clear day, totally unexpected, from a new member of our congregation. He wanted to know whether he was still welcome to worship with us. He and his wife were divorced. That I knew. They were sharing custody of the children and that was going well. But now he had a male partner with whom he was sharing his life, one who loved him and cared for the children too. They didn't want, as he put it, "to make a scene," but he wanted to know what I thought about this and whether they would be welcome to worship with us.

More real people. How do you think I responded to him?

God's amazing love welcomes real people into the community of faith called the church. It is amazing because it is always a larger love than I can manage. Mostly I am happy about that. If God's love were no greater than mine, the church wouldn't be much—just a reflection of me and my limited prayers.

God must love real people because he not only created them, but he knows their sin, pain, and brokenness in ways that I only glimpse from time to time. God welcomes all of us in the waters of baptism, and keeps washing us with mercy and forgiveness. In that grace we keep learning and growing.

Further, God's acceptance of all these real people in the church means that there is room for me as well. To that I add "Amen."

Reflections on the water:
> *perfect in every way*
> *our ideal companion, we agreed*
> *carved from lovely stone*

19. Are We There Yet?

The life of the baptized is like a young child on a long trip. Parents recognize that experience. Let's say our destination is Disney World. In the morning darkness we pack the luggage into the van, push and shove it until it fits. We buckle sleepy children into their car seats. Our journey begins slowly through a very quiet city; then we pick up speed as the morning sun rises on the horizon. Suddenly a pleading voice punctuates the quiet of the morning. "Are we there yet?"

Baptism begins a life journey with Jesus Christ. The water vanishes, but the gift it signals remains with us throughout the journey. We are children of God, an identity deeper and stronger than any trial we encounter along the way. God loves us with an unconditional love, anchored in the cross of Christ and his resurrection. We have the gift of faith, blessed with hope, nurtured in love. The dimensions of this status come clear as we move along in the journey, wondering along the way whether we'll ever reach our destination.

We have the promise *now*; our experience of the full reality is *not yet*. This *now/not yet* situation often leads to tension in the life of a Christian. Hope and expectation alternate with doubt and despair. A Christian lives in a time between times.

This reminds me of Holy Saturday in the church's calendar—that strange, empty time between Good Friday and Easter, that is, between Jesus' death on the cross and his resurrection. In my experience as a pastor, this seems like "down" time, a time for reflection, for sensing the pain of the cross without leaping too quickly to resurrection joy. No matter how much I have worked on my Easter sermon, I think it through again during this time, fumbling through Holy Saturday's emptiness before moving on to God's stunning new moment, Jesus' victory over death. The growing use of the moving Vigil of Easter liturgy in the life of the church will immerse us in powerful baptismal themes and transform our in-between-time struggle to resurrection now.[27] How we yearn to receive this from Christ!

This struggle enters the rest of my life as well. I know that there is more than sin and death, more than the messes of the world and my own failures, so that I long for the Easter word. I await the news of the genuinely smashing truth. I need to hear it again and again. Why? Because I fumble around in an imperfect world, where my life only hints at what it will be. I love, but so imperfectly. I care, but too casually. I reach out, but much too infrequently. I pine for the destination that I have not yet reached.

The longer we live "in Christ" the greater our awareness of the not yet. And yet, it is the greatness of Christ "for us" that defines our Christian life, not our incremental insights. The waters of baptism, more than anything else, underscore this "for us."

Martin Luther experienced the "in between" character of the Christian life in many ways, but never more dramatically than in his nighttime struggles with the powers of darkness. In 1521 his prince provided him sanctuary in the Wartburg Castle, to escape the sentence of death on sight. This was a very difficult time for him. He was unusually productive during the day, translating the New Testament into German. At the same time, he agonized in the hours of darkness, doubting God's mercy and doubting it especially for himself. The devil was so real for him that, when nuts fell on the castle roof, he considered them aimed by the evil one himself. He then cried out his fundamental defense plea, "I have been baptized."[28]

Baptism is not merely an event of the past, but a relationship to live. That is why Luther called out to God. He was summoning God to keep the promise made when he was but a week old. Luther's cry was faith calling out in the darkness and there finding Christ. Even this great reformer was not exempt from the shattering and shaking of doubt. He learned, however, that a believer, in times of doubt and despair, must attend less to self and more to Christ.

I learned this lesson in a time of congregational crisis. We had faced financial shortfalls month after month. Finally, our leaders had to make drastic choices, with painful consequences for staff members: wage and benefit cuts, positions reduced to halftime, resignations and vacant positions. Morale plummeted. Though everyone knew that we could not continue without changes, it was an agonizing time. Despite assurance to the contrary, staff members questioned their value and I my leadership. Yet God was there, in the depths of the questioning, the doubts, and the quest for solutions. I recall trusting in God's presence and praying for it. Others did too, and we consoled one another in this trust. God not only walked with us in this dark time, but led us as well. Slowly, with prayer and discernment, we moved toward new staff configurations. More than that, we moved forward with confidence that these arrangements were right for us and for our goals. We experienced God in our "in-between" times, which is, of course, where we still are.

"Are we there yet?" I am not, nor, I am confident, are you. God washes us in the assurances of baptismal waters so that we can live our way through uncertain times. We are a faith family, awaiting arrival at our destination with varying degrees of impatience. Along the way we have each other, for sober realism and gentle encouragement. Together we trust and pray and dream. Group travel is a gift of God. The community of believers holds us to our hope anchored in the waters of baptism, waters that run clear and deep and strong.

Reflections on the water:

confessing the same sins again

he grows weary of repetition

Does God still hope?

20. Through the Waters

The Red Sea is the boundary between life that was and life that will be. Small wonder then, that Christians see baptism as a passage through the Red Sea. The Israelites entered that Sea in flight from their enslavers and emerged as the free people of God. The Sea opened a way to new life for this community and closed to engulf the enemy.

The journey to freedom was not simple for the Israelites. Doubt and mistrust accompanied them. Moses himself was a reluctant leader. When summoned by God to lead, he had a litany of reasons for refusal. Finally, with reluctance, he allowed God to use him. Moses the simple shepherd had to die so that God could raise up Moses the prophet. He had to walk through the waters of change before he could lead others.

The passage through the Red Sea provides a powerful image for baptism. At the same time, it offers instruction for leadership generally. God, in baptism, underscores a profound human truth: before leaders can change anyone else, they must themselves change. John Maxwell, author of many books on leadership, is emphatic on this point.[29]

This is a significant challenge. One of my own rules for ministry, for example, is that I never ask anyone to do a task that I am not willing to do myself. That means that I don't ask members of the congregation to make calls on new residents in our community if I am not willing to lead by example. This kind of servant leadership has integrity, even though I am not necessarily the most skilled at a given task. If I advise someone not to let their insecurities send them running, I had better demonstrate the same.

I dislike dealing with conflict, so much so that I am even now seeking language that will mask my weakness. The truth is: I avoid conflict whenever I can, and I don't understand people who appear to love it as "spice" in their lives. Yet, as a pastor, if I didn't face the reality of conflict, either with individuals or in the church as organization, the result would be a poorer ministry. The door to change and the gate to repentance and forgiveness often remain closed when we pretend that our disagreements do not exist. So what do I do? I pray for courage and wisdom and then get up and face whoever or whatever I must. Sometimes that means someone right now. Did I mention how reluctant I am to do this? Yet, I cannot pray that others deal with their disagreements if I won't do so myself. This is baptism all over again, and I must plunge into those waters. The amazing thing is that life happens in these encounters.

Parents must also embrace a leadership role. It comes with the territory. Parents are not called to be buddies, who worry whether their kids like them. The parental role is not primarily about entertaining children and satisfying every wish. When parenthood is practiced in that way, it results in children who are self-centered, recognizing only themselves and their needs as important.

So what is a parent to do? Lead! Lead by setting good and firm boundaries. Lead by willingness to make the tough and unpopular decision. I read about a teenage girl left alone by her parents on weekends. Her friends wanted to turn her house into "party central." Her boyfriend pressured her sexually. She remarked, "My life would be easier without all this freedom." She will gradually have freedom, but right now she needs boundaries, which means that she needs parents to set them.

Sometimes we cannot be effective parents unless we assess ourselves and make necessary changes. That may require that we forego some entertainment, examine our drinking habits, or simply take time to talk with our children—changing ourselves before we ask our children to change. That is leadership.

One more example: Michael Jordan is arguably the best basketball player ever. However, he may never have achieved that distinction, had not Phil Jackson been such an effective coach. Jordan had great skills: his running jump shots, amazing fade-aways, the ability to take over a game at the end and put in the winning shot. That's only the beginning. Jackson, however, coached Jordan in a skill he lacked, that is, to be a team leader. When Jordan could not only use his own skills "to the max," but also utilize the skills of his teammates, the Chicago Bulls were on their way to a dynasty. His leadership combined his own great play with the play of his teammates which was now raised to a higher level of excellence. A changed leader changes everything.

The mystery of the Red Sea, and of baptismal dying, is that there's a lot we don't know about life on the other side. When we die to self and our self-centered concerns, we trust Jesus Christ that we will come "through the waters" to a life we can only imagine when we are in the grip of the old one. This is baptismal spirituality that bubbles into all of life.

Reflections on the water:

they need to change now

I made a list and checked it twice

but I'm okay

21. Amazing Beginnings

It's just a novel, I reminded myself. It's a good story, but a story all the same. Reading a David Baldacci novel is hardly the same as reading Scripture. But let me tell you why I was so fascinated.[30]

Sean had blown his job. He had worked for years to move up through the ranks in the police department, until he reached the pinnacle of special services: protection. His assignment was to guard a candidate for the U. S. presidency. The candidate didn't have a chance of being elected. That didn't matter. He needed protection from enemies, including the dangerous friends of persons he had prosecuted as a district attorney.

In one moment everything Sean had achieved was lost. He recalled that he had just stood there, failing to prevent the assassination. Now it was all gone, this perfect future he had planned for himself. Because of his momentary lapse, the candidate was dead, and with him, the future.

That is how it appeared eight years ago when this disaster occurred. It was a terrible time for Sean, a journey through Hell. Yet now he was a happy, contented man. After some time off, he had completed law school. Today life was good. He was amazed how good it was. He and a partner had a law firm, and, though it wasn't as exciting as his lost dream, Sean had a better life than he ever imagined possible.

This was only a novel, as I indicated, but it reminded me of a deeper, more powerful truth of Christian experience. Some years ago, in a conversation with a former teacher and dear friend, we came to talk of death and resurrection. "That," he said, "is what God is always doing."

God makes new beginnings out of our dead endings. Jesus' death and resurrection is about him, but it is more. It is the shock of a new reality. What happened with Jesus will happen with us too. And while it is the story of our death, it is not limited to that. God is doing resurrections all of the time. God gives futures we do not expect, from small things like forgiveness by our spouse to the great gift of another chance at life itself.

Pastors serve a congregation in response to a call from God. That sounds impressive and clear, and I wish it had been like that. There was a time when, because of the stipulations of my Letter of Call, I had to leave a congregation following the resignation of the senior pastor. He was ready to leave; I was not. I was prepared to do ministry there for a long time. But it was not to be. I was angry about leaving. My wife and family didn't want to move. But the moving truck came nonetheless.

Another congregation and community welcomed us. They did the best they knew, but they hadn't welcomed a new pastor in thirty years. This was an unusual experience for many. Despite our smiles on the outside, inwardly we cried at the pain of leaving a community we loved. How would we ever live again! We agonized in our grief by day and lay awake praying about it at night.

God wasn't sleeping, however; God was doing a new thing. As we worked at ministry each day, doing the essentials and pushing to go beyond that, God offered us new life in a place we faced with reluctance. That is God's way, creating beginnings from what seem to us to be endings. Three years into our move, life had changed significantly for us, and so had we. After ten more years, we celebrated a time rich with relationships and accomplishments.

These new futures God offers us are not the ones we envision in our doubts. God brings his goodness to us where we are, even when we are certain that we belong somewhere else. As in baptism, God drowns the doubting me so that a new, faithful and hopeful me may emerge.

Since this is God's way in the world, as my friend reminded me, God's work is often not as private as the personal experience I have shared. The presidential politics of American life provide a couple of very public examples.

Jimmy Carter left office in 1981 under the dark clouds of rampant domestic inflation and a 400-day hostage ordeal in Iran. It was a very painful time for him, and, had he been a lesser man, he might have retired to private oblivion. That was not to be. He became, instead, a world advocate for peace and a very public spokesman for Habitat for Humanity. Arguably, no president in the history of this country has had such a remarkable post-presidency; surely none has enjoyed such a dramatic turnabout.

In the year 2000, presidential candidate Al Gore lost a highly contested election to George W. Bush, whereupon assorted pundits wrote him out of our country's future. However, Al Gore has proven to be amazingly resilient. Since his student days at Harvard, he has cared deeply about global issues. He has now become a major advocate for the moral imperative of dealing with climate change caused by greenhouse gases. He has focused widespread public attention on the issue through his movie on the subject, *An Inconvenient Truth*, a movie the scientific community has welcomed and critics have praised.

Jesus said, "Unless a grain of wheat falls into the earth and dies, it remains just a single grain; but if it dies, it bears much fruit" (John 12:24). Jesus is the grain, for your sake and mine. He is the heart open to the working of God. Thus, as we invest ourselves in the nitty-gritty of this life, death is never the last word. Life is. We think that the order is birth and death. Jesus' turns that order to death and birth.

Reflections on the water:

> *on the page of obituaries*
> *his name did not appear, but*
> *he checked again*

"I am about to do a new thing;
now it springs forth, do you not perceive it?
I will make a way in the wilderness
and rivers in the desert."

Isaiah 43:19

22. Dying to Change

Is anyone "dying to change"? We avoid thinking of death, and not just the end of our lives. The end of anything is a kind of death; it causes discomfort. Thus it is no surprise that change, whether personal or societal, is so painful. Change is an ending, closing the door to the familiar. Change is death. In baptismal spirituality it can also open the door to life.

One May morning, a section of *USA Today* fired my reflection on the pain, the problems, and the possibilities of viewing our world through the fresh waters of baptism. Three articles got my attention: a book review, a medical report, and an essay on technology.[31]

The book reviewed, *Green With Envy: Why Keeping Up with the Joneses is Keeping Us in Debt*, by Shirley Boss, describes how envy has resulted in financial problems that jeopardize the well being of many families. Credit card debts, shopping addiction, and home equity lines of credit often lie behind the superficial appearance of "having it all." Competition with neighbors in the race to have bigger and better things rests on the assumption that such possessions will bring a better and happier life.

Boss exposes this as a fundamental phenomenon of American life. She also provides psychological and self-reminder tools for curbing this materialistic habit. We need this kind of awareness. We also need spiritual recognition. God never intended us to find meaning and happiness in things, and the only proper response to this tendency is to die. That is, we must recognize envy for the evil that it is, admit our inclination to it, and change—death and rebirth.

The second article bears the title: "Study: 73 million Americans have diabetes or are at risk." The writer reviews the familiar observations about our behavior, that our consumption of sugars and fats, combined with little physical activity and exercise, has led to multiple health problems. A study reported in the June 2006 issue of *Diabetes Care* indicates that nearly one-third of Americans either have diabetes or a higher than normal blood sugar level. These numbers have reached epidemic proportions, with the potential of increases in heart disease, kidney failure, blindness, and the need for amputation of affected limbs.

What does this have to do with the waters of baptism? It confronts Christians with the questions of what we can do to change and what is our responsibility for ourselves and for one another. Can we die to personal and family behaviors that contribute to the problem? On a larger scale, will we help to create a culture that works to end such unhealthy behavior?

An article on technology poses a similar question, though in a way that is less familiar to many of us. In "Technology Leaves Teens Speechless" the writer describes how text messaging is changing the lives of young people. Using their cell phones, teenagers, whose parents used to urge them to get off the telephone, are now text-messaging one another. They spend a lot of time each day tapping in messages, without any direct oral conversation with anyone close by, even dormitory roommates. This may end up a non-problem, but it appears to be affecting the ability of teens to participate in normal conversations. The spontaneity of face-to-face conversation or a phone chat is being lost. In the workplace employers are increasingly dissatisfied with the oral communication skills of high school graduates.

Does this matter? That depends on the big picture, what kind of world we want. Do engaging human conversations matter? Do thinking and speaking beyond 160 characters (the maximum text message length) make a difference? Are spontaneity and quality listening among the skills basic to social health? If our answer is "Yes," then we may have to make changes, rethinking technology as a tool and not our master.

The above examples may evoke other responses, but I cite them in the service of using baptismal spirituality as a lens through which to examine our lives, both with respect to individual issues and social concerns. Each of the examples involves both of these dimensions of the human condition. Can individuals change? Can societies or cultures change? It won't be easy. It is as difficult as dying. What makes it possible? I offer a brief and much too simple reply.

We begin with our commitment to truth, the conviction that responsible human action properly proceeds from an accurate description of our situation. For example, what exactly is the status of human health generally in our society? Next, we need hope, the expectation that our efforts at dealing with human problems will make a difference. If we accumulate fewer things, for example, how will our lives be better? Finally, we need a vision of a new and changed world. For example, how will a world of spontaneous conversation be more satisfyingly human than sitting next to each other playing with our cell phones?

Baptismal spirituality sends us into the world with two advantages. In our bond with Jesus Christ we have already died and risen with him. We may not be "dying to change" anymore than the next person, but we have the security of making changes with one who holds our destiny in his loving hands. In baptism we have received all that belongs to Christ, the very kingdom of God. This gives us, as we live in relationship with him, a glimpse of the new creation. We need one another in the community that is the church to clarify this vision and declare it in the public forum of the world as a sign of hope.

Reflections on the water:

watching the wisps

of his last cigarette float away

he breathed deeply

23. Letting Go

"Tomorrow is letting go day, Pastor, so we came to church tonight." I raised an eyebrow in curiosity as I greeted her after Saturday evening worship. She hesitated. "We're moving mother from her big old beautiful home – home all her married life – into assisted living. Dad's been gone ten years now and it's time." "So it's time: is that how she feels about it?" I waited for her carefully chosen words. "Who knows? One minute she's excited about the new place; the next she's threatening to lock herself in the bedroom and never come out. I just wish she'd let go and let God."

"Let go and let God." What a simple and beautiful line – and how terrifyingly tough at the same time. Often I do not want to let go; I want to hang on with all my life. This is understandable, as if I am referring to my life as a roller coaster ride. I hang on because I don't want to fly off into space and perish. Letting go in the baptized life, however, is precisely that we might live. For the sake of life, I must release my grip on life as it is and trust the One who makes me his own in the waters.

A favorite story describes a pre-school child who gets his hand stuck in the cookie jar while sneaking a treat. He twists and turns that hand for release, but he is inescapably stuck. Finally, he has no choice but to cry to his mother for help. After a quick look at his hand and the mouth of the jar, his mother gently says, "You'll be fine. Just open your hand and let go of the cookies." Yes, he'll be fine. He might even receive a cookie from a kind and generous mother.

That is often the story of our lives. We want to have more than we should have. We want to have it all, even if it makes us unhappy or ruins us. We may not know what to do, and mothers are not always available to help us. This is an important spiritual matter at its heart.

Jesus told a story of a farmer so successful that he built a new granary to hold the surplus harvest. That very night he faced death—his soul was required of him. His soul/life had become all about more, having more, keeping more. He never considered when more would be enough, and he showed little interest in how the rest of the world was managing. He was smugly successful, unconcerned with God or neighbor. He didn't loosen his grip until God did it for him.

Possessions are such tricky things. We may consider ourselves basically good, even generous. Compared to the really rich, we come off pretty well. Greed doesn't apply to us. And yet, many among us have two homes while others in the world have none. We build houses double the size of a standard house in the 1950s and long for one even larger. And the story of the little boy and the cookie jar causes me to wonder: is it possible to be greedy with little as well as much?

Christians struggle with these questions and that is good. In my congregation little children often lead the way. On Sunday morning during the offertory they fairly dance their way to place their gifts in the "hungry jar" to provide food for others. Except for the one litle fellow who reluctantly dropped in coin-by-coin-by-coin and lingered long. Letting go has many stories to tell.

One beautiful summer day I met an old acquaintance whose daughter had graduated from high school recently. I inquired how life was going for him. "I've had a terrible time," he confessed. "You wouldn't believe how hard it was when she left for tech school. For all those years I'd been her dad and she'd been my little girl. We talked when she came home from school. She drove the tractor on the farm. We shared so much. Then, one day she was gone. She didn't need me anymore." That is the pain of letting go, launching a child to maturity, letting go of parental responsibilities.

Aging snatches things from us as well, like a thief. My mother has lost her eyesight due to macular degeneration. Slowly she has had to let go of activities that filled her life: sewing, quilting lovely bed covers, reading—especially Bible reading, writing church programs, letter writing to family. How deep the pain of such letting go. Only by accepting limits and letting go is there peace.

No one is exempt from the need to let go. Along life's way others hurt us, whether intentionally or not. Will we nurse our hurt into a grudge and allow the grudge to become a constant companion? Or will we let it go? Harry Emerson Fosdick said, "Hatred is like burning down your own house to get rid of a rat."[32] The cost is too great. Let it go.

The waters of baptism assure us that, whenever we need to let go, we are in Christ and we rise with him. Life will be different, to be sure, but with the risen Christ there is always a good surprise.

Reflections on the water:
> *when his fingers bled*
> *from the grudges he held dear*
> *he almost let go*

24. More Than Our Decisions

Decision-making is at the center of concern for parents and for schools. How could it not be? Our children live in a world in which the pressures of sex, drugs, and alcohol come at an ever-younger age. The adults who mentor these children face their own issues of personal relationships, integrity on the job, and national crises.

How do we decide? How do we arrive at the clarity necessary for making good decisions? Do we make lists of pros and cons for choices? Do we have conversations about consequences? In the midst of all of these considerations, baptism provides us a gift of immeasurable value. Though it offers no easy answers to our challenges, it gives us a center from which we can act with confidence.

In the rite of baptism in my church, after the washing with water, the pastor announces, "Joseph Allen, child of God, you have been sealed by the Holy Spirit and marked with the cross of Christ forever."[33] Child of God; that's who Joseph is. He is a child of the God who created the world, delivered his people from slavery in Egypt, and loved them to new life through Jesus Christ. Baptism affirms this connection and declares to young Joseph that he is a beloved, treasured child of God. The waters will dry, but the new identity will remain.

As he grows, Joseph will receive tools from his parents, his extended family, his teachers, and others that will help him to make good decisions. If he is blessed, those around him will guide him well, from sharing his toys as a child to driving the car when he turns sixteen. Baptism, his anointing as a child of God, provides him an identity within which this guidance takes shape. It also surrounds him with a community of faith, family, friends, and other members of the church who remind him of his identity.

Through study of the Bible, Joseph becomes familiar with the traditions of his faith community, with Israel, Jesus, and the church. He learns that God loves him, that Jesus gave his life for him, and that people of faith live for others and not simply for themselves. He worships, serves, and plays with people whose lives and values have taken shape within a Christ-centered community. What he sees, learns, and practices will shape him and his decisions.

Out of the baptismal waters Joseph will develop character. He will be a person immersed in the values of Christ and Christ's community. When he has decisions to make, he will recall that he is a beloved child of God who in turn loves and lives by values he learned in this community called the church.

If that sounds too idealistic, notice that I am describing the gift given in baptism. God has fully given the gift! God is not taking it back. We may have a sense of incompleteness because we have not lived fully in the gift. We may have given slight attention to our baptism or even abandoned any thought of it. But the gift is still there. Members of the community of faith need to remind one another by word or deed, "I love you, and I want you to know that God loves you. You are a child of God." Such a status shapes who we are and the decisions we make.

I know a family in which the Mom and Dad do not hassle their children about going to worship. It is simply what they do because they are Christians. Mom reminds them, "No, you don't have to go to church. You get to go to church." These parents know that baptism means that they are children of God who are members of a community of faith. That is who they are, and who they want their children to be. It is a dimension of their character. They don't have to decide anew each Sunday whether they will go to worship or not. They go because it belongs to their identity.

Some children I know wear a wristband with the letters WWJD, meaning, "What would Jesus do?" At its best,

WWJD is not merely about making good decisions. It is about coming to know Jesus well and understanding our relationship to Jesus. This shapes the character from which appropriate decisions and behavior flow.

What happened in a French village during Word War II comes to mind. Le Chambon was by most measures an ordinary community. However, in the course of the war the villagers saved a very large number of Jewish people from death at the hands of the Nazis. After the war some scholars studied the community in an effort to explain how and why this happened. Why had they been willing to risk their lives to help people whom they didn't even know? Why did they consider this to be ordinary rather than heroic behavior? The answer was that they knew who they were, that, as children of God, they loved their neighbor even at great personal risk. It was not about heroics. It was about their Christian identity and the character of their lives that was shaped by that identity.[34]

We are the water-washed, Spirit-sealed, baptized children of God. We learn the content of this gift as we live within the community of faith. This does more than influence our decisions; it shapes our character.

Reflections on the water:

whatever he decided

the weight of being right or wrong

did not crush him

25. What the World Runs On

Water is simultaneously ordinary and extraordinary. More water than land covers the surface of the earth, and a mere 2.5% of that water satisfies the needs of life. Life itself is a water-based phenomenon. Our bodies are 71% water and upsetting that balance jeopardizes life. Even the ancient Greek Thales of Miletus observed, "Water sustains all." Loren Eiseley, a twentieth century environmentalist, commented, "If there is magic on the planet, it is contained in water."[35] "Why the World Runs on Water" was the title of the keynote address at a 2006 conference on rivers.[36]

Given the role of water on our planet, it is appropriate to reflect on water as the visible sign in baptism. The waters of the womb birth us into this life; the waters of baptism signal our new birth in Christ. God has chosen water to be the medium of both creation and new creation. Life in general depends on water, from God's Spirit who "moved over the waters ... calling forth life" at the beginning to the waters of baptism whereby we "may be given new life."[37] The grand vision of God's future in Isaiah 35 presents water as the sign of a renewed creation. Creation and new creation; birth and rebirth—God blesses us twice with water.

Wonder and reverence are the appropriate responses to the gift of water. It testifies to the love of God, and praise properly follows our experience of its refreshing graces. Unfortunately, we often take water for granted, opening the faucet without a thought of its special character, until contamination hits our supply and we must purchase it along with our food supplies. Notice the place of water in the creation story of Genesis 1. God sets the untamed waters in their place and makes them a blessing: "And God saw that it was good" (Gen. 1:10). The Celtic tradition, with its lively sense of God in nature, describes the waters as a place where "the eternal seeps through the physical."[38] Water is a sacred element in other religious traditions as well.

Water even leads humans from fascination into philosophy. In her Pulitzer Prize-winning novel *Gilead*, Marilyn Robinson presents as narrator a 76-year-old Iowa minister who is writing letters to leave to his 7-year-old son. In one of those letters he refers to the philosopher Ludwig Feuerbach as having said that God surely chose water for baptism because of its remarkably pure qualities. "Water is the purest, clearest of liquids; in virtue of its natural character it is the image of the spotless nature of the Divine Spirit." The reader senses the delight of Robinson's pastor that Feuerbach the atheist should wax so eloquently about water.[39]

The flood waters following Hurricane Katrina in New Orleans and the devastating tsunami in south Asia, on the other hand, remind us that waters do not themselves save us. The waters are not God; God alone brings us salvation. The waters are part of this complex world in which we live, deeply interconnected with our lives and our brokenness. Yet, not even shocking calamities change the fact that water is a gift, given twice, one of the most intimate of nature's signs that God is faithful and near.

Baptismal spirituality is always a spirituality of response. God acts and we respond. Water, given twice, makes this clear. We respond to our baptism as the water of redemption, and we respond to water generally as part of God's creation. The water of baptism connects us with the family of the church, but it also strengthens our connection with all people and all of creation.

For this reason we hear a call to love the world and care for creation from deep within the sacrament of baptism itself. God who births us with water and with water creates us anew in baptism beckons us to share his love for the world.

Water has a special role in summoning the Christian to care for the environment. Consider the following as examples:

run-off from cultivated fields, chemicals that endanger our drinking water, streams in which pollution threatens the fish, irrigation that lowers the water table, marshes drained for development, and others. An example of response is the movement *Clean Water Action* that seeks to maintain established pollution protections for streams, rivers, and lakes.

These examples highlight a variety of environmental issues and the need for appropriate responses from governments, businesses, and individuals. None of us is in this alone. Water, as it flows from one place to another, defying our efforts to be masters of the world, demonstrates the interconnectedness of all of life.

After a baptism at a Sunday morning worship service, when all have left and quiet reigns, I take the water from the font, carry it outside, and pour it gently on the earth. This is not leftover, wasted water. As it splashes on the grass and glows on the leaves of flowers, I view it as holy water. To be sure, it marked the beginning of new life for the baptized. But it is holy water for the earth as well, a sign of God's love poured over a hurting creation. God calls us to share in that pouring.

Reflections on the water:

holy water in our hands

we pour on the earth

to form sacred mud

"But let justice roll down like waters,
and righteousness like an everflowing stream."

Amos 5:24

26. Spirit Blessed

"I wish I had received the Holy Spirit, Pastor." Deep longing filled her voice. "Why do you think that you haven't?" "Well, I cannot name a time in my life about which I can say, 'The Spirit came to me just then; the power of the Spirit overwhelmed me.' I want to be able to say that." I knew what she meant. I would like to be able to say that too. However, I responded, "Let's talk. Perhaps the Spirit isn't missing from your life as much as you think."

Wouldn't it be wonderful if there were one experience or feeling that assured us, "Yes, you can be absolutely certain. You now have the Holy Spirit." We expect that sometimes. Sometimes other Christians claim that it is the case. However, we cannot contain in such a narrow slot God the Father, Son, and Holy Spirit, in whose name we have been baptized. Infant baptism is a powerful testimony to that.

Suppose you were six weeks old at the time of your baptism, or at least young enough that you cannot remember the event. Your parents may have told you about it so often that you think you can remember parts of it, like the crying fuss you made, but that's far from the experience of the Spirit. You received the Holy Spirit in the washing of baptism in the name of the Triune God. As the pastor placed a hand on your head, you received the Spirit in the prayer asking for "the spirit of wisdom and understanding, the spirit of counsel and might, the spirit of knowledge and the fear of the Lord, the spirit of joy in [God's] presence."[40]

Do you know the greatness of the Spirit's power? That you don't recall the time of your baptism is no cause for regret. Quite the opposite. God is greater than your memory, greater than your consciousness or even your mind. God came to you in the Spirit before you ever thought of God. In baptism God declared you his child. God does not wait to declare your importance until your mind develops or your memory forms. God wants you now, before you long for God. That means that you should never identify God with a certain feeling, or, for that matter, the lack of a particular feeling or experience. God is much greater than that

I recall reading what the Norwegian theologian, Ole Hallesby, wrote about baptism. He argued that God worked in the subconscious life of the baptized infant through the sacrament to create faith in ways that we can only imagine.[41] Considering all that babies learn in the first months and years outside the womb, Hallesby may be right. God works in the living actions of parents day by day, shaping a child's very identity. Who knows what the swaddling, the lullabies, the prayers, and tender words will do to create faith? The Spirit who came in water and word in baptism continues to dwell in the child through the surrounding community of faith. Perhaps deep within the child there is even a memory of the water and words of baptism itself.

We don't need that memory, however. The Holy Spirit is ours in baptism because God makes the promise. It isn't about us. It is about God's faithfulness, even in the face of our human tendency to waver. The hymn title, "O Love, How Deep, How Broad, How High," signals this persistence of God.

The entrance of the Spirit is not entirely invisible. God has given us fellow believers, the church, things we can see, hear, touch, feel, and perhaps even taste. We have water and words, as well as the physical laying on of hands—all clues to the Spirit's entry.

These earthly signs help us to see and believe. As part of our life in the community of faith, we see these signs repeatedly as we pray for the Spirit on specific occasions. Perhaps the rite of confirmation is the most familiar such occasion, with its laying on of hands and the prayer for the Spirit's work in the lives of these young people. Here we return to baptism and the work that God began then.

Congregations look for other ways to return to baptism as well, especially for the laying on of hands and prayers for specific gifts of the Spirit. That occurs when we ordain pastors or send out missionaries. We do it whenever we call people to lives that require specific gifts of the Spirit. Ministries of teaching and healing are examples. The circle is more inclusive when, on Labor Day weekend, the church invites members to come in work clothes for a blessing at the baptismal font.

The rite of marriage is connected to baptism. The couple makes their vows with the community of faith surrounding them in prayer. The pastor blesses them with the laying on of hands, as in baptism, and offers a prayer for the Spirit to fill their lives with the gifts of enduring love and faithfulness. We may even view the bride's white wedding gown as a baptismal symbol, a reminder of the white baptismal gown, a sign of new life in Christ, marriage as a new creation filled with love, hope, and the promise of God. It signals that the Spirit blesses us with forgiveness and new life, both for the future God offers and the commitments to live in that future.

We may not remember having "received the Spirit," but the baptismal truth is that we receive the Spirit repeatedly, especially in the community of faith, but not there alone. God's Spirit comes to us in as many ways as does water itself—like gentle dew or nurturing rain, bubbling springs or meandering river, mighty floods or deepest ocean. The Spirit has blessed us indeed.

Reflections on the water:

hands on one's head

the weight of heavenly blessing

the lightness of the Spirit

27. A New Holiness

A splendid garment clothes the baby presented for baptism. Made with love, perhaps generations earlier, it is a family treasure, dazzling white. Always white. White marks the holiness we have in Christ, not in ourselves. In spite of flaws and failures, we are now in Christ "a chosen race, a royal priesthood, a holy nation, God's own people" (1 Pet. 2:9).

The expectation is that holy people live holy lives. The First Letter of Peter, a baptismal writing, makes clear that the new holiness of baptism summons us to a disciplined life. We must put aside the "desires that [we] formerly had in ignorance"—malice, insincerity, and envy, for example (1 Pet. 1:14, 2:1). New Testament lists that include things like "fornication, impurity, passion, evil desire, and greed" (Col. 3:5) come to mind. We are to die to these, that is, put them to death. This is the dying of our baptismal spirituality. Christ is the model for the baptized Christian. "As [Jesus Christ] who called you is holy, be holy yourselves in all your conduct" (1 Pet. 1:15).

As important as holiness is, however, what we learn from Jesus is not limited to this. For example, if Jesus had been typical of his day, there would be no stories of his contact with lepers. He would have avoided these people. The rest of society kept their distance from lepers since they were ritually unclean, excluded from normal socialization, including public worship. Contact with them made a healthy person unclean as well, even though temporarily. Thus lepers lived in a cold, lonely, and isolated world.

Jesus, however, reached out and touched lepers, shocking his contemporaries. With his compassionate touch he healed the lepers and restored them to the community. Had he chosen to avoid the lepers, others would have understood. They did so everyday, sometimes going out of their way to escape contact. But Jesus walked a new way of compassion. The welfare of lepers mattered more to him than his own cleanness and personal purity.

Jesus acted similarly when he met people with unclean spirits. Such contact made a person unclean. But Jesus did not view that as an obstacle. Other stories that feature this preoccupation with ritual purity are the stories of the woman with a flow of blood and the Syrophoenician woman whose daughter had an unclean spirit. In each of these stories Jesus shifts concern to the welfare of others. This was radical behavior in a society focused on ritual purity. Jesus replaced this with love and mercy for others. Jesus was determined to love lepers, which meant that he touched them and healed them.

This attitude of Jesus was at the center of a major crisis in the early church. What should the church do about unclean Gentiles who wanted to follow Jesus? Could the church accept them, and, if so, on what conditions? The Book of Acts reports the stories that shaped the character of the church from the beginning. Ritual purity was not to be the standard for admission to the community. Jesus himself was the standard—the church was to be a community shaped by love and mercy. People who were once outsiders were welcome in this community, not grudgingly, but warmly, because this was the way of Jesus himself.

1 Peter 2:10 presents a clear vision of the community of faith: "Once you were not a people, but now you are God's people; once you had not received mercy, but now you have received mercy." From this it follows that the church practices the qualities of compassion and mercy that it has experienced. The church is not separate from the world, an isolated club of the baptized. Far rather, it is a community of those who enter boldly into the world, identify its wounds, and show mercy.

The temptation is to view the life and work of someone like Mother Teresa as an exception. Her calling was to minister to the wretched, the dying, the sick and diseased. We admire her for that, but we cannot imagine ourselves doing it. That will not do, however. Mother Teresa was the church at work in just one place. Her life challenges us to be the church in our place.

There are signs that people in the church recognize their vocation to do mercy. For example, a young man dying of HIV-AIDS returns to his parents' home and the congregation of his youth. That wasn't his first choice, but he had nowhere else to turn. At first people are upset and angry, but to their surprise they soon discover a real human being in this ill man, and a fellow Christian as well. They reach out in tender love to care for him, touching him, holding him, even finding a new peace together. When Jesus comes, he does not come alone. Today this congregation has a small, but visible ministry to others like the young man.

All this beckons us to reexamine a line that echoes from our childhood: Cleanliness is next to godliness. On one level this was encouragement to wash our hands regularly and well. On another level it was a way of viewing moral purity. In view of Jesus, cleanliness may not be the best way to characterize this. Though baptized in glistening white robes, we hear the call to live our holiness getting dirty by practicing mercy.

Reflections on the water:

HIV AIDS

an alphabet

that God does not know

28. The Front Line

"Your orders are to report for duty at the front line." We should add words like these to every baptismal certificate. They would make clear that our baptism into Christ calls us into the real world for the battle of our lives.

The "Narnia" movie based on C. S. Lewis's writing presents an imaginative insight into this real world: it is not a neutral place. We hear this in a bit of forest dialogue, when the beavers advise the children to keep their voices low, because even some of the trees are on the side of the wicked witch. The world is a battleground for the powers of good and evil, truth and deception.

In baptism we join this battle on the side of Jesus Christ. We cannot remain neutral. We are on the side of Jesus, who has won the decisive battle when he died on the cross and rose from the dead, the battle that determined the outcome of the struggle between God and "sin, death, and the power of the devil."[42] Jesus has claimed us and put his mark on us. This means that the powers of evil look on us as the enemy. They will target, tease, tempt, and terrify us, seeking to win us over to the dark side. Our very lives are the battleground.

Immediately following his baptism, Jesus entered the wilderness. God's chosen and beloved had no time to bask in the glow of baptismal glory. The Spirit drove him into the wilderness. Baptism pitched him into a forty-day battle with Satan that tested him, shaped him, and prepared him for an even tougher time. His life was the critical point at which the powers of evil either won it all or lost it all. It came to a climax at Golgotha. Jesus won.

If Jesus has defeated the powers of evil, should not our lives as Christians be a breeze? We know that they aren't. The devil will not let it happen. He doesn't know when to admit defeat. He is the punch-drunk fighter who has lost the fight but blindly flails on. He cannot win, but he continues to bring pain, suffering, and misery through all his pointless punching. We would be naïve to think that we might get through life without test and trouble.

This description may seem a bad fit for the baptism of infants and young children. We find it difficult to imagine them as warriors. However, give them a few years and their own imaginations will surpass ours. They will read in Ephesians 6 about putting on "the whole armor of God," and they will be determined to fight. The better we know Jesus, the more clearly we will see the nature of our struggle.

Let's examine a few battlefields in the struggle for our souls.

Parenting is one. Say we baptized your third child, Emily, on Sunday in a service that won your sometimes-questioning heart. Everyone said that it was a beautiful ceremony, even Uncle Bob, whom you had to arm-twist to church. The pastor's sermon was just for you, or so it seemed. Now you are at home again with your family, in that real world. Here you will decide whether you will live the faith that you promised: "to live with [Emily] among God's faithful people, bring [her] to the word of God and holy supper, teach [her] the Lord's Prayer, the Creed, and the Ten Commandments, place in [her] hands the holy scriptures, and nurture [her] in the faith and prayer …."[43] This is not just about Emily. It is about you, her parents, and your forming of the "holy habits" (as the Methodists say) that will be a model for her. Baptism is a wonderful gift, but for parents to bring a child for baptism and then neglect Christian practice themselves is to offer faith with one hand and take it away with the other. Parenting is a battlefield.

Our life as consumers is another. Have you noticed the full and overflowing garages in our neighborhoods? If our cars could talk, they might inquire where their home went. They've been left out in the cold. Advertising presents us with a spiritual dilemma, suggesting that our next purchase will fill us with happiness and satisfaction. Our response may resemble that of our children, "If only I get [you name it], I'll never ask for another thing again." That is, until the next time. We cannot satisfy our souls in this way. Our purchases cannot give what God alone can give.

Citizenship is another battlefield. Many Americans have begun to question the war in Iraq and struggle to clarify their own positions. Others view such disagreement and dissent as unpatriotic. We who belong to the community of the baptized, however, know that we have a citizenship greater than that of our country. We are citizens of an eternal kingdom over which God rules. That kingdom challenges all earthly kingdoms, even the land we love, and calls us to the struggle for truth and justice.

When tempted to withdraw from these battles, I remind myself that these are the places to which Christ summons us in baptism. Dietrich Bonhoeffer observed that "peace must be dared," because safety is not the same as peace at all.[44] There is a strange comfort in finding our lives in the swirl of battles with temptation, struggling to do good, daring to believe, caring about truth. The struggle affirms that our lives matter. A cheap and easy peace indicates that we have surrendered to alien powers. On your own front line of battle, ponder that strange comfort. Then trace the sign of the cross as a baptismal reminder that you live and move in the power of Christ.

Reflections on the water:

> *party on without a care*
>
> *answerable to no one*
>
> *when the Devil's in charge*

29. Thinking Differently

The comedian Flip Wilson exposed a weakness of our humanity in an old act. Caught in his own trap with nowhere to turn after wrongdoing, he pleaded earnestly, "The Devil made me do it." As though that got him off the hook! This was a comic act, but we who laughed at his dilemma recognized ourselves in it. We saw the truth: when it is to our advantage, we pose as helpless victims, maneuvered by an outside force to do what we didn't want to do. In fact, we cooperate with the Devil, playing along when we know that we could and should resist.

The Apostle Paul offers advice on baptismal spirituality in his letter to the Romans: "So you also must consider yourselves dead to sin and alive to God in Christ Jesus" (Rom. 6:11). We live our new life in God's grace, Paul insists, and sin no longer rules us. Grace rules. Does this mean that we can go on sinning, exploiting God's grace? No, for in that case we have misunderstood what our baptism means. We have died with Christ, and then we rose with him. This is a beginning, our new future.

What does it mean to be dead to sin? One way to understand these words is that sin cannot separate you from God. Sin lacks that power. You can live your life secure in Christ. Another way, built on the first understanding, is that it has to do with how you think about yourself. To consider yourself dead to sin is to view yourself as a person who does not respond to sin's lure and power.

Recently I was driving in heavy traffic, moving from two lanes to one. Impatient drivers crowded around me. Most of them showed consideration for other drivers, but a few raced ahead, determined to break into line on ahead. One darted in front of me, narrowly avoiding my left front bumper. Was I pleased with this? Were the words forming on my lips "full of grace"? Not likely. I was angry. Words I didn't use circled like vultures in my mind. Steam rose from my head. But then I shook my head and thought to myself: What is happening with you? You don't have to feel this way. This anger is not you, not the new you God has made. Let it go. I did, grumbling at first, and then I let the grumbling go. I put a CD in the player and let the music calm me.

This is a trivial example, to be sure, but it reminds us that the struggle continues even though we have died to sin in baptism. It is as though the Devil is making a desperate effort to hold on to us. This will continue until we are completely new in the kingdom of heaven. The grasp and grab of the Devil are pointless at the end, for we live in Christ.

That is why "consider yourselves dead to sin" is a new direction for our lives. Instead of remaining the helpless victim, we have the chance to adopt new patterns. We are free to give up the old "stinking thinking" and face our tests with the confidence of knowing that Christ is for us and in us, making us new.

This is not pop psychology, another example of "self-help spirituality" that we can buy off the newsstand at the supermarket. This is acting in faith as the new person that God has made us. This new person is still a sinner, flawed but forgiven, acting on hope that is based in Jesus Christ.

We all face temptations, things that bring out the worst in us. We need to use our heads and stay away from those situations if possible. I know a young girl who seems always to get into big trouble when she hangs out with a certain friend. It is as though her mind goes bonkers in the chemistry between the two of them. In time she will learn about herself and what it is that leads to such behavior. But for now, stay away.

The same advice applies to the man tempted by Internet pornography. If he is dead to sin, he must avoid typing into his computer the search words that will lead him where he should not go. He needs to halt the self-justification and rationalization that opens this path.

Part of us, the dead part actually, enjoys the journey down these salacious paths, and the world offers us an ever greater variety of them. Considering ourselves dead to sin means that we will admit the lure of these temptations, and then take responsibility for our lives. Sometimes we can simply remove ourselves from the source of temptation. In other situations we may need counseling or spiritual direction from another person. The point is that we must do something. Though we are sinners, in Christ we are never helpless victims.

When we interrupt our old thinking and take a new turn—that very time can be an incredible experience of being alive in God. We did it, not because of our own strength, but because we took a chance on living in the power of who we really are, the children of God. We did it, and it feels shockingly good, like a plunge into the icy waters of Lake Superior after a sauna. We are alive, alive in God.

Reflections on the water:

> *revenge kept her rolling on*
> *until the day she got off track*
> *by forgiveness*

30. Into the World

"Pastor, it must be great to serve God like you ministers do!" How is a pastor to respond to that? One might say, "Yes, it sure is, and I wish everyone had the chance." On another day it could be, "It's not really as wonderful as you suppose, especially after a month of too many crises and late night meetings." An alternative answer, with a focus on the common life of the baptized, would be, "It's a terrific calling, but it is no more than the vocation you have in the world. That is the gift of baptism."

Baptism is ordination for all Christians. Perhaps better, it is the rite of lay ministry. The church is a community of ministers, some of whom serve in positions of ordained leadership within that community, but most of whom spend their lives in service in the world. Though it risks becoming an empty cliché, church bulletins have it right when they head the staff listing with "Ministers: All the Baptized." The primary challenge for the community of believers is to focus their energies on ministry.

Consider Jesus' baptism by John in the Jordan River. God proclaimed him "Beloved" in the waters, just as happens to us in our baptism. Jesus received the Spirit in baptism, as we do in ours. Then the Spirit drives him into the wilderness where he faces a testing that is the prelude to his mission. Baptism is not the end of his spiritual journey; it is the beginning, the plunge into the harsh realities of life—the challenges and temptations, and his work in the world. Jesus does battle against the forces that rise up against God. His work was in the world.

Martin Luther was an advocate for the work of God in the sacrament of baptism. The baptism of infants was not a problem for him, since God was the primary actor in the sacrament. God can bestow gifts of forgiveness, life, and salvation when and where God chooses. In fact, Lutherans will argue enthusiastically that justification by grace alone is never clearer than in the baptism of infants.

At the same time, Luther insisted that all of the baptized, at whatever age, become part of a community with a mission. They are not only the "beloved"; they are the "beloved disciples" as well. By the grace of their baptism they become followers of Jesus, his disciples for the world. There they will be the people in whom the Spirit lives, whatever their place in society.

With one of his typically earthy examples Martin Luther remarked that a milkmaid is living out her baptismal calling by milking the cows and feeding the calves.[45] Such chores are "in the world." They are "of the earth," just like the waters of baptism itself. When those waters flow from the heart of God into the font and then into the world, the love of God flows with them. Gabriel Fackre identifies the place of the baptized person as wherever in the world there is room for service, because Jesus himself was a servant.[46] "For the Son of Man came not to be served but to serve" (Mark 10:45).

So where in the world do Christians live out their baptism? Anywhere, and in whatever roles they fill. Sometimes we choose those roles; at other times we find ourselves in a role we had not counted on. Each such role can be a calling from God.

Father Roland Rolheiser anchors our life in the world in the paschal mystery, that is, in Christ's suffering, death, and resurrection. He describes parenting, for example, as a way that Christians live out the calling of baptism to die and rise with Christ, or, in other words, to lose themselves in service. When newly married, husband and wife find joy and delight in each other and have eyes only for each other. When they have a child, their focus changes. They must serve this helpless newborn at convenient and inconvenient times, 24/7. There is no escape. God gives these two people an opportunity to learn parenting, and thereby to live as the baptized. In spite of themselves, they will rise in the middle of the night to feed the child or change a diaper. Through this dying to self-interest God shapes them to conform them to Christ as servant. In the process they become a family in which love blesses life.[47]

In *The Cost of Discipleship* Dietrich Bonhoeffer writes, "When Christ calls a man, he bids him come and die."[48] That's enough to make one want to turn and walk away, or perhaps run! We often do precisely that. However, our vocation in the world shapes us even against our will. A parent, for example, may not want to get up to comfort a child, but does so nonetheless. It feels like dying, doesn't it? Luther observes that we should not seek our own dying, but that every calling provides ample opportunity for trouble, suffering, and the submission of self.[49] In those moments God is shaping us to be the person that we became in baptism. God is, in those moments, blessing others with the service that we provide in spite of ourselves.

Think of those times when it fell to you to do the hard duty. You might be the police officer assigned to visit a home and tell a wife that her husband has died in a car accident. You might be a representative in the state legislature moved by conscience to cast a vote that will cost you dearly in a future election. Or in retirement, with the luxury of few obligations, you choose to mentor a fourth-grade child in the after-school reading program.

Baptismal waters flow in one direction, into the world. That is the direction of the baptized life, into the world. "God so loved the world" (John 3:16). Whether the profile of our service is low or high matters not. What matters is that, in Christ, we become waters of life ourselves.

Reflections on the water:

coffee, toast and eggs

she places them with grace

a morning communion

31. Restless Hearts

"You have made us for yourself, O Lord, and our hearts are restless until they rest in you." [50] These familiar words from Saint Augustine's *Confessions* may not connect with us as we glide along on the choppy or still waters of life's surface. In our ordinary experience, we may not recognize that the sense of emptiness within us crying out for more is a spiritual voice. We may miss in that emptiness the echo of the voice of God beckoning us home.

Nevertheless, could it be that waters themselves bear an echo of the eternal God, a lure for a thirst we cannot name? The question arises from the attraction of water in our lives. Every weekend vacationers take to the waters, as though a magnet were drawing them. We don our swimsuits and race to the beaches of quiet lakes and roaring oceans. We grab our fishing gear and drive through the night to spend a few treasured days bobbing on the waters of a pristine lake. We swim or sit in a chair on the beach, enjoying the blue-green waters sparkling in the morning sun. This renews us. We come alive. We sense a peace that feels even spiritual.

Psalm 42, on noting the drawing power of water for wild creatures, compares it to spiritual longing. "As a deer longs for flowing streams, so my soul longs for you, O God" (Ps. 42:1). The deer seeks water to satisfy thirst, but humans long for more. We understand the longings of the deer—raging thirst after the chase, desperation in a rainless season—because we ourselves run dry. Water alone will not satisfy us, however. To be sure, we delight in a shower or a drive to the lake, and recognize the healing powers of water for aches and pains. But our restless hearts long for more. Nature alone does not satisfy. We long for God.

Robert Frost reflects on water in another form—snow. In the poem "Stopping by Woods on a Snowy Evening" he pondered the darkness of his journey and acknowledged that "the horse knows the way to carry the sleigh." Such is life in nature's kingdom, and that is a comforting gift. It is not so simple for the driver, however, who has "miles to go before I sleep," and then the haunting echo, "miles to go before I sleep."[51]

Perhaps, as mentioned before, Celtic spirituality has it right, that the eternal seeps through the physical. This is certainly true of our longings. For Christians, however, it is in the particular waters of baptism that we glimpse the eternal and hear a response to our deepest longings. The waters of fishing streams and peaceful lakes are pointers, but they are not our home. These waters hint at the healing of our hearts and of our world, but we find wholeness in God who uses water to restore us to him.

The water that has given us Christ in baptism reminds us of our connection to the world of nature. We cannot escape this world, and we ignore it at our peril. The waters all about us in nature offer connection with all creatures, even with the wonder and fragility of creation itself. But the waters of baptism connect us with Jesus Christ, God's gift for the mending of our broken world. As in John's vision of a new heaven and a new earth, "the river of the water of life" flows from the throne of God and of the Lamb (Rev. 22:1).

"No Jesus, no peace. Know Jesus, know peace." Though cynical about "bumper sticker Christianity," I find in these words testimony to a central truth: that Jesus grants to restless hearts a peace that the world cannot give. We are made for the something more found in Jesus, his life, death, and resurrection. The waters of baptism bring Jesus into our lives, that we may come to know him and the God who sent him.

The peace that Jesus gives is not a simple peace.

To know Jesus is to know that we are beloved, loved by God. We, who at times cannot tolerate ourselves, are loved.

The waters of the baptismal font declare this clearly. If we hear the word there, we will hear it echoed in the meandering stream and the majestic sea. The waters of baptism give us the name of the one who gives us peace in all those other waters. Our longings find their center and their home in the waters of the font.

To be sure, as long as we live, our longings will not disappear. We will still hang our hopes in the wrong places. We will delude ourselves. We will face disappointments. In our restlessness we must listen to the Psalmist who directs us to "hope in God." Both our longings and our disappointments bear the persistent cry that "my soul longs for you, O God" (Ps. 42:1).

This is deep listening, the most important listening that we do. It brings us face to face with the cross of Jesus. There, in the presence of the greatest love, we die to our stubborn way and rise to the freedom of a joyful life. We will be "like trees planted by streams of water, which yield their fruit in its season" (Ps. 1:3). Our restless hearts have found their home.

Reflections on the water:

the stream gurgled

echoes of a voice I had missed

ripples of truth

Endnotes

1. Martin Luther, "The Large Catechism," in *The Book of Concord: The Confessions of the Evangelical Lutheran Church*, trans. and ed. Theodore G. Tappert (Philadelphia: Fortress Press, 1959), 441.

2. Thomas H. Troeger, "Water Feeds the Fire: Mystery and Metaphor – An Exploration of Poetic Form in Baptismal Texts," *Reformed Liturgy and Music* XXIX, No. 1 (1995): 13.

3. Maxwell Johnson, *The Rites of Christian Initiation* (Collegeville, MN: The Liturgical Press, 1999), 366.

4. James F. White, *Protestant Worship Traditions in Transition* (Louisville, KY: John Know Press, 1989), 44.

5. Gordon W. Lathrop, "Baptismal Practice and the Global Map," *The Lutheran Theological Seminary at Philadelphia,* March 5, 2002, <http://www.ltsp.edu/reflections/2001-2002/020305lathrop.html> (May 16, 2007).

6. *The Haiku Anthology – Haiku and Senryu in English*, ed. Cor van den Heuvel (New York: W. W. Norton & Company, 1999), xi.

7. *Evangelical Lutheran Worship* (Minneapolis, MN: Augsburg Fortress, Publishers, 2006), 230.

8. *ELW*, 230.

9. "St. Patrick's Breastplate," *Byzantines.net*, <http://www.byzantines.net/saints/st-patrick.htm> (June 29, 2007).

10. Dietrich Bonhoeffer, *The Cost of Discipleship* (New York: The Macmillan Company, 1959), 36.

11. *The Gospel of Judas from Codex Tchacos*, ed. Rudolphe Kasser, Marvin Meyer, and Gregor Wurst (Washington, D.C.: National Geographic Society, 2006), 43.

12. *Lutheran Book of Worship* (Minneapolis, MN: Augsburg Publishing House, 1978), 77. All liturgical references in this chapter are from this page and Setting Two beginning on p. 78. A similar but not identical pattern can be found in *ELW*.

13. Johnson, 61.

14. William Kuhns, *In Pursuit of Dietrich Bonhoeffer* (Garden City, New York: Image Books, 1967), 117.

15. Eberhard Bethge, *Dietrich Bonhoeffer – Man of Vision, Man of Courage*, ed. Edwin Robertson (New York: Harper and Row, 1970), 830.

16. *ELW*, 95-96; similar in *LBW*, 77.

17. *Cost of Discipleship*, 57.

18. James Wallis, "What the Waters Revealed," *Sojourners Magazine*, November 2005, <http://sojo.net/index?action=magazine.article&issue=sojo511&article=051110> (May 9, 2007).

19. *ELW*, 330.

20. *ELW*, 231.

21. Glenn L. Borreson, "Toward a Baptismal Discipline: A Study in the Theology of Dietrich Bonhoeffer" (MTh thesis, Luther Theological Seminary, 1978), 26.

22. Borreson, 33. This reference is very important, giving the community almost a sacramental quality for Bonhoeffer.

23. Brad Hesla, "A Dazzling Bouquet," in *Global Songs 2: Bread for the Journey* (Minneapolis: Augsburg Fortress, 1997), 28-29.

24. *LBW*, 48; *ELW*, 87.

25. *LBW*, 77; with variation, *ELW*, 94.

26. Dietrich Bonhoeffer, *Life Together*, trans. John W. Doberstein (New York: Harper & Row, 1954), 30.

27. *ELW*, 266-270.

28. Roland H. Bainton, *Here I Stand: A Life of Martin Luther* (New York, Abingdon Press, 1950), 367.

29. John C. Maxwell, *Developing the Leader Within You* (Nashville: Thomas Nelson Publishers, 1993), 42. In this instance Maxwell writes that "We cannot lead anyone else further than we have been ourselves."

30. David Baldacci, *Split Second* (New York: Warner, 2003).

31. The three articles are from *USA Today*, May 30, 2006, pages 7D, 7D, and 1D, respectively.

32. *The Westminster Collection of Christian Quotations*, comp. Martin T. Manser (Louisville: Westminister John Knox Press, 2001), 160.

33. *ELW*, 231.

34. Philip P. Hallie, *Lest Innocent Blood Be Shed* (New York: HarperPerennial, 1994).

35. "Water and Spirituality," St. Louis Earth Day 2001, *"Our Waters, Our Rivers,"*

<http://www.cosmicexpress.com/earthday_site/docs/message.html#giver> (June 30, 2006).

36. Jared Diamond, "Why the World Runs on Water," 2006 International Conference on Rivers and Civilization, <http://www.rivers2006.org/html/diamond.htm> (June 30, 2006).

37. *ELW*, 230.

38. J. Philip Newell, *The Book of Creation, An Introduction to Celtic Spirituality* (New York: Paulist Press, 1999), 24.

39. Marilynne Robinson, *Gilead* (New York: Farrar, Straus, Giroux, 2004), 23.

40. *ELW*, 231.

41. O. Hallesby, *Infant Baptism and Adult Conversion* (Minneapolis: The Lutheran Free Church Publishing Company, 1924), 46-52.

42. *ELW*, 1162. This "unholy trinity" is the common enemy of God in Martin Luther's *Small Catechism*, included in the Evangelical Lutheran Church in America's 2006 hymnal.

43. *ELW*, 228.

44. Mary Bosanquet, *The Life and Death of Dietrich Bonhoeffer* (New York: Harper & Row, 1968), 145. Bonhoeffer spoke these engaging words at a 1934 ecumenical conference in Denmark as Hitler was consolidating his power.

45. Gustaf Wingren, *Luther on Vocation*, trans. Carl C. Rasmussen (Philadelphia: Muhlenberg Press, 1957), 9.

46. Gabriel J. Fackre, "The Baptismal Encounter," *Lancaster Theological Seminary Occasional Papers No. 1* (Lancaster Theological Seminary: Lancaster, Pennsylvania, 1962), 31.

47. Ronald Rolheiser, *The Holy Longing: The Search for a Christian Spirituality* (New York: Doubleday, 1999), 200-201.

48. *Cost of Discipleship*, 79.

49. Jonathan D. Trigg, *Baptism in the Theology of Martin Luther* (Leiden: E. J. Brill, 1994), 97.

50. *The Confessions of Saint Augustine*, trans. Edward B. Pusey (New York: The Modern Library, 1949), 3. The line quoted is a typical modernization of the old English translations.

51. *The Poetry of Robert Frost: The Collected Poems*, ed. Edward Connery Lathem (New York: Henry Holt, 2001), 224-225.

Appendix: How to Use This Book

1. As individuals

As I indicated in the introduction to *Water for Your Soul*, my hope is that you the reader will experience this book rather than speed-read it. The value of the spiritual haiku that concludes each chapter is dependent on such meditative reading. The thirty-one chapters naturally make for a one-month experience in baptismal spirituality.

2. In partnership

A close variation on this individual reading is doing your reading with a spiritual partner such as a friend, a spouse, or another person you trust. My suggestion is that you each do your own reading and reflecting for about a week, one chapter a day, and at the week's end, meet together, compare notes, and pray together. I would especially encourage you to share personally where the spiritual haiku may have taken you. Again, the introduction provides suggestions to guide your meditating.

3. Within the congregation

Pastors and congregational leaders may find this book helpful in several other ways. Parents can be encouraged to use it either before or after the baptism of their infant or child. Either timing has advantages and disadvantages, but the value of both is increased with accountability. For example, parents can be led to 1) do the readings in partnership with each other, or better yet, with other parents, 2) meet with the pastor on a schedule of his or her choice, or 3) gather several times with other parents of children being baptized under the leadership of the pastor or congregational member. The month's worth of readings makes three to five gatherings a reasonable number. Variations on this approach can be helpful with adults preparing for baptism, too.

Another possibility is to encourage households to read the book as a congregational discipline. Doing about five readings a week from Ash Wednesday through Holy Week would accomplish this during Lent, or four or five a week during the seven-week Easter season. Let me add again for emphasis: whether individual or group use is chosen, both this book and baptismal spirituality are meant to be experienced, in other words, to be God's *water for your soul.*